clueless

Ten things I wish I knew
about Motherhood
before becoming a Mom

Kerri Weems

Printed in the United States of America
First Edition: September 2011

ISBN-13: 978-1-54392-698-9

Cover design by Megan Burns
Cover and Author photos by Natalie Broach Photography

Contents

1   **Introduction**   Who Am I Now?

5   **Thing #1**   The Perfect Mother is a Myth

19   **Thing #2**   You Must Have a Strong Sense of Identity

41   **Thing #3**   Everything Is About to Change

57   **Thing #4**   To Work or Not to Work?

73   **Thing #5**   Your Body Will Never Be the Same

91   **Thing #6**   Learn to Live Life in the Margins

107   **Thing #7**   Step Back for the Right Perspective

121   **Thing #8**   There is No "Right Way"

137   **Thing #9**   Your Sex Life Will Never Be What It Was: It Will Get Better!

151   **Thing #10**   Your Children Are Only Young For a Season, So Enjoy It!

165   **Conclusion**   You Can Do This!

Introduction

Who Am I Now?

Identity—the sense of who you are. You spend the first two decades of your life trying to answer the question, "Who am I?" And just when you've reached a manageable idea of what the answer could possibly be, life blindsides you with a new season that challenges who you thought you were—or who you imagined you would become. For me, the identity-ambush/ interruption came with my transition from "wife" to "mother."

After having my first child, my daughter, Kaylan, I experienced an 18-month bout of post partum depression. It was one of the darkest times in my life. Part of what contributed to my struggle during this time was that I did not know what to expect as far as real lifestyle changes were concerned. Everyone told me having a baby would be the most wonderful thing in my life and every moment would be precious. Other moms told me how they had revelations of God's unconditional love in a way they knew would be impossible outside of motherhood. In hindsight, all those things are absolutely true; but, I was unprepared for the complete and immediate shift that took place when my little bundle arrived. I can't say I would have avoided passing through the valley of post-partum depression had I known "My Big 10." However, I think being armed with some understanding of what to expect could have helped me mentally prepare for the onslaught of powerful and conflicting emotions I encountered.

On the one hand I was obsessively in love with an adorable baby girl. I loved her in a way that was completely different from the way I'd ever loved anyone. On the other hand, I actually resented her arrival because it took from me my much-valued freedom. I have always loved to travel, stay out late, and come and go as I pleased. I resented being tied down because my days were determined by her needs. Yes, of course I had expected that I would have to give up my own desires to a degree, but honestly I was never prepared for the extent of sacrifice that was required.

I wanted to be a great example of a Christian mother; so I tried my hardest to fulfill the laws and requirements set forth for the constitution of a "virtuous" wife. Here's the problem: I hated it. I felt constrained, lonely and resentful, and in every way ill-suited for such a life. I truly admired those women who had chosen to live in such a way and did it with joy and effectiveness. Yet I could not embrace it as the finality of what I was called to do.

Let's face it; I had major issues with Christian motherhood. Some of my issues were truly because of my own personal limitations. I needed to grow in love and sacrifice. I needed to learn to rest and stop striving so much. But some of my issues were a response to an ideal of motherly perfection that I could not and did not wish to live up to. The road to separating the "traditions of men" from "the law of love" made for a long and complicated, but ultimately satisfying journey. Through it, I learned what God requires of me is not always what makes its way into books and teaching series. I also discovered that just because something finds its way into popular parenting magazines does not mean it is right or brings honor to God.

Somewhere between the pages of the Bible, talks with mature women who had walked this road before me, and the love and support of a too-good-to-be true husband for whom I cannot be grateful enough, I found me, the mother. I found that embracing who I am makes me a better mother. So, I work. I write. I put my kids in daycare and sometimes leave them with sitters when I travel. I don't play dolls or do crafts. I do read with my kids. I teach them how to think. I take every opportunity to show them how to apply the word of God to their lives. I obsess over my closets being organized, but I couldn't care less about the dust on my tables. I don't go to all of their school parties and I don't carry around a video camera. Our lives are built around God, His church, the Great Commission, and the Great Commandment; and everything else falls into place where it should be. I have learned what is good and what the Lord requires of me: to do justly, to love mercy, and to walk humbly.

As I've talked with my friends along their own journeys into the season of motherhood, I've noticed some recurring themes in our conversations. I've developed a list around those themes I call "My Big 10." These are the ten things I believe should be in a user manual that comes with your first baby. Every new mother passes through a season of trying to find her new self—the mom self. I am sure that most, if not all women in every stage of life, hold themselves up to a few standards, which they cannot realize, an image of perfection they were perhaps never meant to attain. I don't want to tell anyone my way is the right way. I simply want to encourage women to seek God first, to find the freedom to be who God created them to be, and to embrace the joy in each quickly fleeting season of life, be it motherhood or some other key transition.

Thing #1

The Perfect Mother is a Myth

I could hardly wait for Kaylan, my 4-year-old daughter, to wake up. Surely, she was going to take one look at my masterpiece, start jumping up and down, and totally forget how frustrated she was with me last night because I wouldn't let her help me with her class project. To wrap up the unit on apples, her teacher had asked all the moms to bring in some kind of apple dessert to share with everyone; the choice was up to each mom: sliced apples with a tub of caramel, apple cookies, apple sauce, even an apple pie. But as I gazed down the horizon of *my* apple dessert, I could pretty much guarantee that all the others would pale in comparison. And I don't use the word "horizon" lightly because this dessert required a 4-foot long tray in order to properly display each treat.

Today was my debut as a pre-school mom, the first time my child was required to bring the class something from home, and I was determined not to let my Kaylan down. Granted, I was a bit of a kitchen-nazi last night when she tried to assist me in rolling out the all-organic, whole wheat, made-from-scratch piecrust needed for each apple turnover, but I just couldn't take any chances for imperfections. It was a good thing she was deep in sleep at 2 a.m. when I started making the homemade frosting because there probably would have been no way to keep her from wanting to help me pipe each letter onto the turnovers. But I knew once she saw this tray of 26 homemade apple turnovers, each with its own letter of the alphabet, she was going to be so proud of her mama! And did I mention these were all-organic, *as well as* low-fat, low-sugar, and heart healthy? They were a sheer gourmet triumph of nutrition-y apple goodness.

I had just finished applying the extra concealer under my eyes (I couldn't let the other moms *know* I had been up all night; it would blow my "Perfectly Put Together Super Mom" image) when I heard Kaylan bounding down the stairs. I waited for a bit so I could overhear her gasp at the sight of the turnovers, but not long enough to give her the time to reach up and actually touch one. She was happy, and I was ecstatic (possibly induced by sleep deprivation and over-caffination). All that was left was to figure out how to carefully transport this 4-foot long tray of ABC turnovers to her classroom without denting or scratching any of them. It wouldn't be an easy task, but it was too late to turn back now.

I made sure to leave with plenty of time for driving very slowly and taking each stop and start with great caution. *I wonder what all the other moms will be bringing?* I thought as the other cars on the road were zipping to get around me. *I hope they don't feel bad when they see my dessert.* I decided it would be best to play the whole thing off very nonchalantly, so as not to intimidate the other women. "Oh, these little things?" I'd say breezily, "They're just something I whipped up at the last minute."

Finally we arrived at school, and my angel Kaylan opened up every single door for me to carry the long tray into her classroom. We got there just in time to start the apple dessert frenzy, and I proudly presented my *piece de resistance* for all to enjoy. All the other moms gave me great compliments as the children marched through with their plates, filling them up with the many different apple treats. As I looked around, I was actually quite surprised at the number of dishes that literally *were* thrown together at the last minute: apples sliced on plates with jars of peanut butter or caramel sitting beside them, a couple of store bought apple pies and cookies, and one mom had just brought a bowl of sour apple Jolly Ranchers! As Kaylan and I sat down to eat our desserts, I have to admit, I was feeling pretty good about my turnovers. Let's just say, if this apple day were a contest, I felt pretty good about my chances of coming in first place. I started to feel really embarrassed for them as I sat down next to Kaylan to eat our desserts... but not nearly as embarrassed as I was about to feel for myself.

I looked down at Kaylan who was chewing on something with her face all scrunched up. "These are yucky, Mommy," she said matter-of-factly. Fully expecting to see one of those store-bought, sugary, processed apple cinnamon cookies in her hand, I was shocked to see that instead it was her Letter "K" apple turnover! The one I made—with no sugar, whole wheat, no preservatives—at 2 a.m.. WHAAAAT?! I quickly snatched it from her and tasted it for myself. Sure enough, once the bit of sweet icing melted away, my mouth was left with a dry, cardboard-like flavor and a very, very, very chewy crust. I could've cried. In fact, when I looked around the room at all the trays of demolished treats, the only ones left uneaten were mine. I could still see all the letters of my ABC turnovers scattered on plates throughout the room which could only mean one thing: nobody else liked them either. My all-night baking extravaganza ended up filling an entire wastebasket. Nice.

I had a looooooong conversation with myself on the drive home. *What was I thinking? I don't even like to bake. From now on, anytime my kid needs to take anything to school, I'm going to buy it at the store, and it's NOT going to be organic! Who was I trying to impress? What image was I attempting to live up to? Did I really think these turnovers would somehow prove to everybody—including myself—that I've mastered this "mom thing?"* And on and on the self-analysis went.

This was the day I realized I had been buying into the Myth of the Perfect Mother.

WHAT IS THE MYTH AND WHERE DOES IT COME FROM?

If we were really honest with ourselves, when asked what we think makes up the "Perfect Mother," most of us would say: She is like June Cleaver—an amazing multi-tasking genius who is able to keep her house immaculate while cooking every meal, handling all the grocery shopping, completing all the laundry each week (washed, dried, folded, put away *and* the socks matched with no remainders), and still has the time to emulate Martha Stewart by planning arts & crafts for the kids. She has the body of an athlete and works out four times a week. In addition, she attends every school function, volunteers for every fieldtrip. She grinds her own bread, makes her own baby food, and assembles perfectly nutritious gourmet lunches for each child to take to school. She is like Mother Theresa with her humanitarian efforts, has time to pray and spend time with God, and makes sure each child has quality one-on-one time with her. *And* she gets the entire house put together before 8 p.m. so she can run up to bed and freely share some intimate time with her husband (the guy she adores, never fights with, and always submits to gracefully). Oh yeah, and she does all this with her hair and make-up perfectly done at all times. And she smiles all the time and never loses her temper. And she never overeats. And she always vacuums in high-heeled shoes. And, and, and....

This is the myth, and it's a big, fat fantasy. Whose fantasy? I actually can't imagine, but nevertheless, many of us buy into it. Is it any wonder so many women feel frazzled and overwhelmed by motherhood? Any sane person should understand that the job described above is humanly impossible for one woman to accomplish, right? But again, if we dared to be honest with ourselves, many of us are plagued with guilt because secretly we believe this myth could one day become our reality if we just continue to work hard enough, or be organized enough, or learn to say "no" to just the right things.

I know I did, and now I am so glad I've been freed from that madness! If only I had realized this *before* I stayed up all night baking those ABC apple turnovers.

THE MYTH IS A MYTH

The #1 Thing I Wish Someone Would Have Told Me Before I Became a Mom is that the perfect mother is a myth. It is a ginormous lie and will never be *anyone's* reality. When we stop to logically consider this June Cleaver/Martha Stewart/Mother Theresa/Angelina Jolie amalgam of perfection, we can see how ridiculous it really is. Take for example, the preconception that the perfect mother can *only* attain that status by laying down any other activities or employment that are outside the confines of parenting and homemaking. That is fabulous for the woman who makes this choice; but, what about the woman who decides to go back to work while her children are still young, or the woman who chooses to hire outside help for the cooking, cleaning, and childcare? Are these women to be deemed less-than-perfect moms? Of course not! And yet that darned myth still seems to haunt us.

In truth, the picture of this myth was invented during a very isolated time in history. It wasn't until the Post-World War II era that American women as a whole had the luxury of staying home with their children on a full-time basis, tending solely to the affairs within the four walls of their homes. Before this we women—other than the elite, upper class society—were

*Elaine Tyler May, Homeward Bound: American Families in the Cold War era, (New York: Basic Books, page 11)

right along with the rest of the world, working in the fields with babies on our backs, tending to farms, working in careers afforded to women, or assisting our husbands in their desired trade.[1]

The television broadcast of *Leave it to Beaver*, beginning in 1957, gave us this ideal of the Caucasian, middle-class family, along with its image of the perfect mother, which began to take root in our society. Hollywood reinforced that unrealistic standard in films and television that followed, and the American woman immediately started trying to live up to it. (Some things never change, do they?) By the late 1960s, the Women's Liberation Movement began, and the pendulum began to shift in the opposite direction, except, it seems, within the Christian Church. This June Cleaver image was hailed as the pinnacle of womanhood for most of my youth. The problem is this: the things of God are always trans-generational, trans-cultural truths that can span throughout time. The things of this world usually do not offer timeless truths.

Please don't misunderstand me; I am in no way implying that the woman who chooses the career of Stay-at-Home Mom is wrong or "less than." On the contrary, it's a true God-calling that takes amazing patience, stamina, and a whole lot of hard work! I have great admiration and respect for these incredible moms. But being at home is only *one* of the myriad God-callings He has for each one of His daughters. As Christian women, if we limit God's work in our lives by believing there is only one cookie-cutter destiny that each of us must accomplish, we will only become frustrated, dissatisfied and discontented with our lives. We must trash the myth that there ever was or ever will be *one particular* image of the "perfect mother," and instead allow God to lead each one of us along our own distinct journey of motherhood.

When we look to the Bible to help us form our image of the ideal mom, we find they were just as human back then as we are today. Those biographies are every bit as flawed as anything coming out of Hollywood. Think about it: Moses' mom put her baby in a basket and plopped him in a river. Did she even do a test run first to make sure the thing could float? What kind of a mom does that?! Verdict: not a good mom. And then there's the widow Tamar who disguised herself as a temple prostitute and seduced her father-in-law in order to conceive an heir. How would you like to be the boy in class whose mama was a prostitute? Verdict: not a good mom. And what about Abraham's daughter-in-law, Rebekah, who favored one twin son over the other? She helped her son, Jacob, trick her other son out of his own birthright. Or Leah and Rachel who were in pregnancy wars, trying to see who could bear more sons? Or Bathsheba, the mother of Solomon, who cheated on her husband while he was valiantly fighting in battle? And I'm not even going to bring up the Old Testament moms who, in extreme famine, literally ate their young. Talk about desperate housewives! Verdict: NOT good moms.

Before you get discouraged, know this: there is hope. God certainly doesn't want any of His girls bumping around in the dark trying to figure out this motherhood thing; and, as always, the answers *can* be found in His word. They just might require a bit of careful study to uncover them.

BETWEEN THE LINES

After my apple turnover fiasco, I had a real heart-to-heart with God. I realized I had some strongly ingrained preconceptions of what it meant to be a "good" mom along with very unreal expectations for myself in this arena of life. I was tired of feeling guilty, tired of feeling like a failure, and totally ready to learn what God's ideal for being a mom is. I determined to scour through the scriptures and form a model from what I found in the Bible, and *only* from what I found in the Bible. At first, I was a bit frustrated because I went to what I thought were the obvious places—stories of actual Biblical moms. But as you just read, many of those turned out to be pretty dysfunctional scenarios. (On a side note, though, I was very encouraged that despite many of these mothers' obvious imperfections, God's grace on their lives and the destinies of their children were realized. How much more will His grace cover ours as well?) It didn't take long for me to discover that finding God's ideas and descriptions of womanhood would mean reading between the lines. That's when I found the indispensable resource of the book of Proverbs.

The book of Proverbs is also widely referred to as the Book of Wisdom, and from the first chapter to the last, Wisdom is personified as a woman. How significant, in a thoroughly patriarchal society, that these Holy Scriptures, originally written by men to be studied primarily by men, would personify an entity as integral as Wisdom in the feminine sense. From the very first verses, we can hear the pleading words of King Solomon as he upholds Wisdom to be the very key to living a successful life. As I read through Proverbs and learned what Wisdom looks like, what she brings to the table, and how extremely valuable she is, I began to build an internal picture of who I was as a woman and what I could aspire to be.

Over the next several months, Wisdom became my mentor and role model, and she still leads me today on my pursuit to become the woman God created me to be. As I studied Wisdom throughout Proverbs, she taught me how to frame a tangible picture of what a true woman of God looks like. I realize, at first, this might seem a bit esoteric, so let me explain.

Proverbs 1:7 teaches us that the fear of the Lord is the beginning of wisdom; in other words, the starting point of my journey to being a woman of Wisdom is complete reverence, awe, and submission to Jesus. Any question I have in life, any direction I require, is found when I engage from a posture of the fear of the Lord. If I don't start there, then I won't ever find authentic wisdom because real truth lies only in God. As my mentor, Wisdom urges me to frame my image of a godly woman with a foundation of the fear of the Lord.

In Proverbs 3, Wisdom paints such a beautiful picture of womanhood, way better than any "perfect" mother stereotype we might envision. In verses 13-18, the writer of Proverbs describes Wisdom as more valuable than silver or gold, more precious than rubies, and nothing desired can even compare with her. (Do you think this about yourself?) He continues by writing that she holds long life in one hand and riches and honor in the other. She leads people down delightful paths, and all her ways are pleasant and satisfying. (Would your friends say this about you? Your kids?) Also, she is life-giving to everyone around her, and happy are those who hold her tightly.

(Would your husband say this?) This is the kind of woman I want to emulate.

Another of her attributes is found in Proverbs 14:1, "The wise woman builds her house, but the foolish pulls it down with her hands." (nkjv) This one really hit home for me as I searched to find a composite picture of womanhood in God's Word. I asked myself: *Do I build up the household of my life with positive words and actions, or do I rip it apart with criticism, complaining, and sarcasm? Am I building up my self-image, or am I constantly thinking and talking negatively about my body, my work, my role as a wife, mother and friend? Am I building up my husband, or am I tearing him down with nagging and finger pointing? Am I strengthening my friendships or am I undermining them through gossip and comparison? Am I helping form great confidence in my kids, or am I overbearing and controlling?* I realized I definitely wanted to be a woman of wisdom, one who is continually building her house, not a foolish one destroying it with her very own hands.

After spending significant time in the Book of Proverbs, I became extremely thankful that there wasn't a plethora of specific female role models in the Bible. Had there been, I may never have searched and found such a beautiful, stately mentor as Wisdom herself! My favorite part of what I learned is that there is no description of this Wisdom woman's physical appearance. Even in the climax of Proverbs in which the last chapter describes the famous "Proverbs 31 Woman," there are no adjectives describing her age, weight, hair color, or cup size. All her characteristics focus on internal matters—her integrity, her work ethic, her leadership, and her entrepreneurial abilities, her legacy, and her honorable reputation. It's all about her character. What a relief not to have a physical standard to follow.

I know so many women who say they'd give anything to be twenty-five again just so they could have their nice supple body back; but, as for me, I'm going for the image of this Proverbs 31 Woman. I'd never want to go back to my mid-twenties again because it was way too much trauma to gain the wisdom I have within me today. I wouldn't trade my 40-year-old soul for the perkiest butt in America. It's just not worth it. And one of those wise truths I have gained in my 40 years is that, while there is a myth of the "Perfect Mother" alive and well in the minds of women today, it is indeed just that: a myth. The only "perfect" thing God's word encourages His daughters to find is His good, acceptable, and perfect will for our lives. And this perfect will is unique and exclusive for every single one of us.

Do you suffer from PMS?

That is, Perfect Mother Syndrome. Here is a short list of symptoms:

- Do you daily feel guilty about not doing enough with your kids?
- At the end of each day, do you collapse on the couch utterly exhausted?
- Do you always feel as though you are the one who needs to provide the homemade treats for the classroom?
- Do you feel guilty when you are at work because you are not with your kids?

- Do you feel bad when you are with your kids because you're not accomplishing the tasks on your 'to do' list?
- Are you always trying to do seventeen things at once?
- Do you ever text, drive, *and* apply makeup simultaneously?
- Do you feel guilty every time you feed your family take-out?
- Are you always thinking about what you could be doing better?

If you answered "yes" to 5 or more of these questions, you very well could be suffering from the PMS!

Here are some simple steps to recovery:

- Stop. Breathe. Pause. Breathe again.
- Admit to yourself that you are striving for an impossible standard.
- Make a short list of the things you do well and enjoy doing.
- Tell yourself daily, "Good job!" when you accomplish these things.
- Make a short (or long) list of the things you don't do well.
- Forgive yourself for not being perfect. And then do it again because you really didn't believe it the first time.

Find creative ways to lean into your strengths and delegate your weaknesses. For instance, if you love to cook but hate to drive your kid to and from practice each day, offer another mom free meals in exchange for her chauffeur services. If you hate to organize but love to do arts & crafts, find a mom who is the opposite; you can teach her kids to craft while she organizes your pantry. Think outside the box! Stop feeling guilty. Although, once you've mastered this, you will then need to learn to stop feeling guilty about not feeling guilty... and so it goes.

Thing #2

You Must Have a Strong Sense of Identity

I love the show *What Not To Wear*. It has every bit of entertainment a girl needs: fashion, drama, suspense, trendy hair and makeup, an occasional bit of romance, and most of all, shopping for new clothes and shoes. Seriously, what else do you need for a good show?

It's so much fun to watch the make-over process as these people get transformed from ugly duckling to gorgeous swan in just a matter of a few minutes (well, a few minutes for the viewers, that is.). And then, we wait with bated breath for the big reveal when the participant finally gets to strut her stuff with her new clothes, new stylish look, and new attitude. The reveal is my favorite part, and is what compels me to watch this show every chance I get. I love seeing how Stacy and Clinton, the show's fashion gurus, teach everyone (including me!) what the newest trends are and how to incorporate them into any person's budget *and* body type. However, there was one time when the WNTW team was WAY off. I remember watching this pivotal moment, and could not believe what I was seeing. I even started yelling at the TV, "What were ya'll thinking?! Why even air this episode?"

This particular show began typically enough, with pictures of a put-together college student. She was the kind of girl who took the time to dress perfectly every morning while the rest of us showed up to class in our sweat pants and bed-head. Then they showed pictures of her current look. My, my, how the tables had turned! In every shot, she had on baggy, mismatched sweat suits (complete with spit-up stains) and not a hint of makeup on her face. But the worst part of her appearance was without a doubt, her hair. It looked as if she had not cut or styled it since those college pictures were taken. It was long, scraggly, and hung all the way past the high waist and unfortunately-placed pockets of her mom jeans.

Maybe I could have understood her attachment to her Rapunzel-like tresses if they had been... well, pretty. Or super shiny or even curly, but this was definitely not the case. All thirty-seven inches of her mane worked against her—the color, the (lack of) shape, the limp and thinning waves at the bottom, the dark greasy roots at the top. She had become completely enveloped by her own hair. Ladies, I'm not trying to be catty here, but I would bet there are many of you reading right now who would have been just as tempted to sneak up with a pair of scissors and whack off her hair yourself! I thought, *Even if those stylists don't change anything else, if they can just get to that hair it will make a world of difference. It will change her whole appearance!*

With this kind of starting point, the team had their work cut out for them. But I had seen them work their magic on challenging cases before, and I was confident their usual genius would prevail. They would wave their magic wands, and *POOF!* this woman's transformation would be nothing short of incredible. I could not wait to see her reveal at the end of the show so I sat on the edge of the couch, captivated, as the show opened up her life.

This "fashion failure" was the kind of gal any of us would like to have as a friend. She was a great mother of four kids under the age of eight and totally devoted to her family, friends, and community. She shared, however, that somewhere along the path of motherhood and service, she'd lost track of herself. She couldn't remember the last time she went shopping for adult-sized clothes, and she told the cameras that even if she did venture into a mall, she'd have absolutely no idea what to pick out for herself. I had to admit, she had some legitimate challenges. Being a tall woman just over 6', she had always found it difficult to know what styles were right for her body. I loved watching her reactions as Stacy and Clinton cleaned out her closet of old t-shirts, sweatpants, and ill-fitting jeans; her face was a combination of relief, excitement, and hesitation. But even as they were helping her buy new clothes, I couldn't wait until the team got to hair and makeup.

I was getting so anxious to see the final result, I fast-forwarded through all the commercials (thank God for DVR!) so I could quickly get to the best part. This woman's husband, children, sisters, and best friend were at the party awaiting her transformation. The camera crew was interviewing them, and they were visibly excited and anxious to see how she would look. Then suddenly, a hush fell over the crowd. The moment had arrived. It was time to see the transformation of this frumpy, hippie mama into a much hipper, trendier, and younger-looking version of herself.

And then she walked out.

Total shock! My jaw hit the floor, as did every person's at the reveal party. This woman strutted out in an amazing night-on-the-town dress, stunning jewelry, and crazy-hot shoes. Her make-up was gorgeous and she looked just perfect... except for her hair. It was EXACTLY the same! Her way-too-long, scraggly, dirty-blond catastrophe of a hairstyle was just as it had been at the very beginning of the show. She let them change everything about her appearance, except the very worst part. The disappointment was palpable, and I thought everyone seemed really awkward as they complimented her appearance. It seemed as if no one wanted to state the obvious, but everyone was thinking the very same thing: *Why didn't they do something with her hair?*

"What is going on?" I actually said out loud. "What was the point of all this, if she wasn't going to let them cut her hair?! Why'd they even put this episode on the air?" I was so frustrated that I grabbed the remote and shut off the TV. "Well, that's forty-five minutes of my life I'll never get back." (Although in truth, it was much more than forty-five minutes because I couldn't stop thinking about this woman and talking about this episode with all of my friends.)

This woman had been given a once-in-a-lifetime opportunity to have a team of experts—free of charge—give her a complete beauty and fashion make-over, and she was unable to let go of the very thing holding her back the most. They could have done nothing more than cut her hair and the transformation would have been dramatic. Instead, she refused to allow them to do anything *at all* to her hair; not even trim off the inches of fringy, scraggly split ends. She told the hairstylist she loved her hair the way it was, that her hair was who she was, and it would be impossible for her to let go of it. This woman had lost herself in her hair, somewhere between shoulder-length and past-the-bottom length. More importantly, she had gotten so lost in her identity as an always-on-the-go mommy in sweatpants, she couldn't begin to imagine herself as a sexy wife or the trendy friend anymore.

I thought about how, in the not so distant past, I had found myself feeling a bit how this young woman must have felt. Just weeks after my second child was born, I remember walking by the full-length mirror in my bedroom and thinking, *Whoa! What happened to me? Have I even showered today? Or yesterday, for that matter? And when was the last time I put on my make-up? Come to think of it, where is my make-up?* My reflection that day compelled me to make these personal promises: I am not going to allow motherhood to swallow me. I am not going to get so overwhelmed by the daily activities of being a mom that I lose sight of the real Kerri.

Which brings us to the #2 Thing I Wish Someone Would Have Told Me Before I Became a Mom: You must have a strong sense of identity. The truth is, if you don't have a firm grip of who you are before you have kids, motherhood can encompass and consume you.

Here is what I mean: Imagine a big tent. Your identity is like the set of various poles needed to keep that tent standing up, nice and taut. When it's time to enlarge your tent, you need to reposition the spikes, stretch the fabric, pull the ropes tight and stabilize the poles, ensuring the entire structure doesn't collapse on itself. If the poles are strong and deeply embedded in the ground, everything is fine. But if they are splintered, weak and wobbly, or only hold a shallow grip in the ground, as soon as the stretching takes place, the poles will collapse inward, making a great big tent mess.

Motherhood is 24/7 and can be overwhelming at times. It's challenging, and it most definitely stretches a woman to her capacity (and I don't just mean physically!). In many ways, motherhood forces us to "reposition the poles" of our identity as we enlarge our capacity to contain the incredible blessings and changes that children bring into our lives. For the one who walks into this season with a strong identity, an accurate view of her values, gifts and talents and a positive self-esteem, motherhood is an exhilarating addition to her life. It empowers her and completes her. Through the shifting and enlarging of her life "tent," her self-image is sturdy enough to handle the stress of the changes. She'll say things like, "I didn't know I could have this much patience." Or, "I never dreamed I could love another human being this much!" Or, "Wow. I'm a killer multi-tasker!" But for the one who becomes a mom without first gaining a real sense of who she is, motherhood can devour her. Instead of simply being an added facet to her life as a whole, she BECOMES motherhood and can begin to lose sight of anything else. Her poles have fallen in, and she's all wrapped up and struggling within this tent called maternity.

It doesn't have to be this way. Motherhood is an amazing privilege and one of the most fulfilling destinies we can experience. No matter where you presently find yourself along this mommy path, you can fully embrace and love this season of life, but it definitely takes a clear and strong grasp of your identity.

WHAT IS IDENTITY?

Your identity is your sense of self, your perception of who you are, and how you define "you." If you were to sit down and thoughtfully describe yourself, what kind of adjectives would you use? What activities are you good at, which ones come naturally to you? What is your outlook on life? What frustrates you and why? What are your passions? What are your dreams? When you have a strong sense of your identity, these questions are easy to answer. And, these answers help you understand why you act, react, and feel the way you do.

But what if you have trouble answering these questions? Or what if you can only answer them with negative responses such as:

- The adjectives that describe me are impatient, stressed, and kind of pessimistic;
- I don't know what really frustrates me or makes me feel happy;
- I'm not sure what I hope for the future—I just hope it's not bad.

Sometimes, it's easier to answer questions about ourselves by naming what we are *not* rather than what we *are*. However, when we only think of ourselves in terms of what we are not, we are unintentionally creating our identities in a negative space. In other words, we are eliminating characteristics from our identities, but we are not claiming for our own anything worth keeping. When you base your identity on what you are *not*, you end up with a vacuum, leaving nothing solid to build upon and expand.

Now, it can be helpful to *begin* forming our identity by knowing what we aren't; but, if we want to have a strong identity, we must move beyond that. We must be able to articulate who we *are*. That means defining ourselves in terms of positive statements:

- I am persistent;
- I am a positive person;
- I am organized and disorder makes me feel frustrated;
- In the future, I want to get a college degree, move up to management, or open my own business.

Look at the difference between the list of negative statements and the list of positive statements. Even the language of the positive statements is stronger. But there is something else, too. Speaking about ourselves in positive terms makes us accountable to a certain extent. It compels us to take ownership over who we are and what talents and gifts we have been given. I think facing that may be scarier sometimes than living in the comfortable ambiguity of negative space.

There have been times in my life when I was actually

surprised by my response to certain circumstances. I've found myself asking questions such as: *Why am I reacting this way? Why does this make me feel so stressed out? What do I really believe about this situation? What do I feel about my capacity to handle it?* It was not until I was able to assess *in positive terms* what I truly believed about myself that I discovered the long-term personal growth I desired, as well as the ability to actually embrace my God-given identity with confidence and joy.

If we choose to walk through our entire lives with an underdeveloped sense of identity, never truly examining who God made us to be or what He purposed for us to do, our lives will be lived in a vague way. Our expectations for the future will be cloudy at best and, therefore, remain unfulfilled. However, we can maximize our efforts to become all we were created to be when we take the time to look inward—remember where we came from, consider where we see ourselves going, evaluate our gifts and talents, and assess the types of personalities we possess.

WHERE DID YOU GET THAT IDEA?

Self-examination is extremely important when it comes to defining our identity. The messages we tell ourselves each day—the beliefs we hold about our marriage relationships, our views on motherhood, our roles as friends, and our contributions to our communities—all these positive or negative thoughts running around in our heads have come from somewhere. We hold on to many of them and they, in turn, hold us up like the poles holding up our tent. Yet some of them we are desperate to change. Just as we need to understand the source of both the positive and negative ideas, we must know where we came from to be able to move forward in the direction we want to go

To run toward our future destiny without gaining an accurate picture of our past would be like going to Mapquest for directions and entering only the address of our destination. Nothing would happen. We must first enter the address of our current location, enabling the program to offer us the most effective route. Obviously, we don't want to set up camp in the realm of our past, but it is often advantageous to take an active glance backward in order to gain perspective on how we landed in our current place in life.

When Stovall and I first started Celebration Church, I spent some time doing pastoral counseling. Often, I'd meet with married couples in a crisis. They were desperate for someone to help guide them to a place of success in their relationship. Many times, they'd be arguing while I was attempting to help them communicate. With one particular couple, weeks went by as we worked together to figure out why they were having so much trouble getting along. All of a sudden, three months into our counseling journey, the wife casually mentioned, "Oh, yeah, and when I was a child, I was sexually abused." She stated this as if she were giving me the color of her living room carpet.

I couldn't believe that while we had been plowing forward, working so hard to make some progress in the restoration of their marriage, it had taken her three months to bring up such an enormous factor. She blurted it out as if it was no big deal, the very issue that had been impacting their marriage the most. When approaching the path toward healing, this revelation should have been the starting point.. Instead, so much time had been wasted detouring down side roads. The problem? They had a clear destination in mind for their Mapquest of marriage counseling, but had failed to provide an accurate point of departure. The result was they were all over the map, trying to carve out a path for restoration. It wasn't until they went back and started from home base that they were able to truly move forward toward success.

If you have never taken time to evaluate why you are the way you are and why you believe the things you believe, this next section will give you four main influencers to determine your personal "starting point."

IDENTITY BUILDING BLOCKS

1. Family of Origin. What was the environment of your childhood home? Did you have both parents in the house? How did they express their love to you? Was there divorce? Abuse? Abandonment? What is your birth order? There are aspects of your identity that have been formed by your family of origin. Some of these may be very positive. Others may be negative. Most of the time, it's a little bit of both.

In my family, I am the older of two children. When I was nine years old, my father passed away from brain cancer. With my younger sister being only four years old at the time and my mom working through her own grief, I had to grow up a little faster than I probably would have otherwise. Looking back now, there is no doubt that the experience of my father's death during those very formative years had a tremendous impact on my identity. I began to see myself as a caretaker, a stabilizer. I felt responsible for my sister, and one of my most valued character traits became that of being "low maintenance." As strange as it may sound, I am thankful for having developed those traits, as they have served me well throughout my life. However, they also came with a few pretty big blind spots that set me up for unwelcome surprises in other areas.

2. Life Experiences. If you were to create a timeline of your life, which experiences would you tag? How did they alter your thinking, your beliefs, and your self-esteem?

In college, I chose a relationship with a man who was emotionally abusive. While he was a Christian, he definitely had some serious relational issues because he was constantly telling me how ugly and stupid I was, how no man would ever want to marry me, and how lucky I was that he found it in his heart to put up with me. Even worse than the way he treated me was the fact that I allowed him to do it. I believed what he said, and I stayed in the relationship for two years.

Once I finally left the dysfunction, I had to stop and take a hard look at why I let this guy treat me like dirt in the first place; otherwise, I probably would have ended up with the same kind of guy the next time around. I realized that my life experiences had caused me to build beliefs and assumptions about myself—and about men—that were totally untrue.

Because my father died when I was very young, I didn't have a strong male influence in my life. Throughout my teenage years, I had a lot of guy friends and was seen as the "buddy" type, not the girlfriend. I actually had guys say to me (more than once), "If I wasn't already dating (insert girl's name here), I would definitely be into you." Ummmm... Thanks? I think. Maybe they were trying to be sweet in their own dorky high school boy way. I'm sure they meant well. But the message I heard was, "You're a great second." Remember Ginnifer Goodwin's character in the movie *He's Just Not That into You*? She was always trying to find reasons for why the guy she liked was not pursuing her: *He's shy. He's busy right now. He's too focused on work. He's travelling. It's summer time.* Uh, yeah... that was me. So during this time in my life I started believing that I would always be second best. I came to believe that no guy would ever be "into me" enough to choose me first.

Of course I realize now that my melodramatic high school dating life was fairly typical. I mean it wasn't like I was mistreated or I was some kind of outcast. But the truth is, I formed beliefs about myself through those experiences. It's funny how our beliefs drive our actions, and our actions lead to outcomes. Without realizing it, I had come to believe that I was always going to be second best. That set me up to believe that I was lucky to be with that abusive college boyfriend, even though he treated me badly. I look back now and wish I could just slap that former me for believing such lies. Once I finally did some self-examination to understand why I was making these choices, I was able to change those wrong beliefs about myself.

We all have had "things" happen to us throughout our lives. Some major. Others minor. And it is through these experiences that we draw conclusions about how these "things" have shaped us. So often these assumptions are negative; but it's only when we have taken the time to examine the "what's" and "why's" of our lives that we can begin to build the kind of identity we truly desire.

3. Aptitudes. Where do you naturally excel? What are your strengths, natural abilities, and talents? What hobbies or activities do you enjoy? If money was not an issue, what career would you choose? What are the dreams in your heart that never seem to fade? Your answers to these questions will lead you to your aptitudes.

When we utilize our aptitudes to help us accomplish projects and goals, we can build our identity in a positive way as we gain a sense of value and experience success within ourselves. Certainly, we can get out of balance if we allow our aptitudes to become the totality of who we are, like the successful athlete who gets injured and now feels he has no purpose for life, or the mom whose children are all off to college and is now completely unsure of what to do with the rest of her life. But when we embrace our gift and talents and allow them to become part of the fabric of our lives, we can then use them to build strong self-esteem and self-worth.

God has given every one of us unique aptitudes, and they are directly related to our destiny and purpose here on earth. If you are unsure of yours, this is not an area to approach passively. We live in a culture that preaches and promotes the dream of being "discovered." The popularity of shows such as *American Idol, So You think You Can Dance,* and *America's Got Talent* attest to our love affair with the Cinderella story of discovering a great talent hidden amongst common humanity. But what I've learned is that it's actually extraordinarily rare for raw talent to propel people to success. The older I get, the more life I live, and the more of the world I see, the more I am convinced that successful people are focused, persistent, and intentional. Rarely does someone's "all of a sudden" actually happen that suddenly. There is no such thing as an overnight success. In the majority of cases, what we see is a snapshot, a single moment of years of hard work.

Please don't sit around and wait for someone else to recognize your strengths or "discover" your gifts and talents. Discover yourself, yourself! You can actively frame your future if you will take the responsibility of understanding what facets of your personality are unique to you and in what areas you excel. Read books that can help pinpoint your strengths. Take online personality tests to help you recognize what careers are ideal for you. At the end of this chapter, I will point you toward several resources to help you in this discovery. Be an active participant in discovering your aptitudes!

4. Core Beliefs. What are the true beliefs you hold in your heart? Not the beliefs you *say* you have, not the beliefs you *want* to have, not even the beliefs you *act* like you have. Core beliefs are the values and assumptions deeply rooted in your heart, and they work as an internal compass guiding you through life. Every day, we walk through life making unconscious decisions about how to respond to and how we feel about the situations we encounter. Most of these decisions and responses are based on the core values we hold. We rarely act in opposition to them; and, when we do, we feel conflicted and frustrated.

For instance, if you have a core belief that you will never be successful, then no matter how hard you try, you probably will never live in the fullness of success. And even if you do achieve your goals, you'll still find yourself feeling unfulfilled and uncomfortable because that success is actually in conflict with what you believe at your core. Generally, if you never address the incongruities, you'll eventually do something to sabotage that level of success. Likewise, if you have a core belief that you are a bad mom, then regardless of how well you adapt to motherhood, you will always feel guilty, as though you are never doing enough. You will worry constantly about your children's future. On the other hand, if you own a core belief that you'll most likely succeed at anything you try, then whether it be your career, motherhood, weight loss, marriage, finances or friendships, you probably will find a way to accomplish whatever you set your hand to.

Family of origin, life experiences, aptitudes, and core beliefs are four ingredients that weave together intricately to build our identity. However, of these four factors, our core beliefs are the most significant because we have the most power to change them. We cannot alter our family of origin, there is nothing we can do about our past life experiences and we can only enhance our aptitudes, but we *can* change our core beliefs about all of these three, as well as of ourselves and of our futures. If we examine our hearts and discover that we hold beliefs that are flawed or even false, we actually can renew our minds and learn to change them. We *can* build the strong, positive identity we need.

DECONSTRUCT TO RECONSTRUCT

No woman (or man, for that matter) has the perfect identity or image of herself. Even if she did, she would have to reassess that perfect identity regularly. Our identity is built throughout our lifetime, with layers being added here and removed there; it is continually morphing into who we are today and into who God has designed us to become. And for all of us, there are facets of our identity that need to be discarded forever. As with the woman I described from *What Not to Wear*; she needed to forever discard her long, stringy hair so the real and beautiful woman beneath could emerge. By the same token, I needed to trash my belief that I would always be second best so God's truth about who I really was could become part of my new identity.

We all need to fight aggressively to align our identities with the woman God sees in us. All our lives, the world has conspired to build our sense of self for us, and that false identity, along with our experiences and the consequences of our choices, have carved beliefs deeply onto the tablets of our hearts, some right and some wrong. The only way we can sift through these ideas and know which ones are true and which ones are false is to hold them up against the Word of God. The messages we tell ourselves should align with the messages God gives us in His word. If they don't, we must cast them aside—deconstruct what we have built up in our hearts—so we can reconstruct our identity according to what God intended.

The Apostle Paul is a fabulous example of a person who was willing to lay down his entire identity to be utterly deconstructed by God. Once he came to know Jesus, his one desire was to know Him and be like Him, and if that meant losing everything he had once considered valuable, so be it. He wanted nothing to stand in the way of building his true identity in Christ.

In Philippians 3:3-10, Paul urges the church not to place any confidence in their own flesh or in their own works. In other words, in any of their manmade identities. He reminds us that the focus of our salvation and the fabric of our identities must rest solely upon the work of Jesus and who He is inside us. Then, he makes himself an example to prove his point:

We put no confidence in human effort, though I could have confidence in my own effort if anyone could. Indeed, if others have reason for confidence in their own efforts, I have even more! I was circumcised when I was eight days old. I am a pure-blooded citizen of Israel and a member of the tribe of Benjamin—a real Hebrew if there ever was one! (Family of Origin) I was a member of the Pharisees, who demand the strictest obedience to the Jewish law. (Life Experiences) I was so zealous that I harshly persecuted the church. (Core Values) And as for righteousness, I obeyed the law without fault. (I'd definitely call that Aptitude, a true gift of discipline!) I once thought these things were valuable, but now I consider them worthless because of

*what Christ has done. Yes, everything else is worthless
when compared with the infinite value of knowing Christ
Jesus my Lord. For his sake I have discarded everything
else, counting it all as garbage, so that I could gain Christ
and become one with him. I no longer count on my own
righteousness through obeying the law; rather, I become
righteous through faith in Christ." (NLT, parentheticals
mine)*

Notice his willingness to disregard each of the four Identity
Building Blocks we talked about earlier. While he was unable
to change his family or origin, his life experiences and even
his zealous persecution of the early church, he was able to
change his core values, *"Yes, everything is worthless when
compared with the infinite value of knowing Christ Jesus my
Lord."* He has discarded as garbage every element that used to
compose his identity for the express purpose of allowing God
to reconstruct his true identity in Christ.

In order for us to build the kind of identity strong enough to
support the tent of our lives, we must have Paul's attitude and
humility. If we want to be able to stretch and grow throughout
our lives and have the capacity for adding huge components to
our identities such as marriage and motherhood, it's crucial to
understand who we are in Christ. The "poles" of our identity
must be our relationship with Jesus, our desire to know Him
more intimately, and reflect the image of who He is. Just as
Paul came to the place of knowing that everything he thought
amounted to nothing, we must come to God with the courage
to surrender ourselves and everything we brought with us.

Because it is only in that nakedness, in that space free from all our exterior trappings that we can begin to discover who we really are and who God has designed us to become.

Also take note, God did not leave Paul deconstructed. Although Paul voluntarily threw out his old identity, God didn't let him move on throughout life with a flimsy notion of who he was. Quite the contrary. The more Paul released and the more he pressed into God, the more of the strength and power of Christ he was able to access. As we read about the amazing pioneering work of Paul—and the massive persecution he faced because of it—it is clear he possessed an unbreakable confidence of his identity in Christ.

Let's look back one more time at our *What Not to Wear* friend. She really did face some challenges with her height and shoe size. Those larger dimensions make shopping pretty difficult for a woman. The whole ordeal was quite emotional for her. She worked hard to obey the rules, and she shed a few tears of frustration and anger along the way. But she kept her chin up and left with some great items, custom tailored for her frame. She looked amazing and she deserved every minute of it. This woman worked hard to fully cooperate with the stylists... until she sat down in the salon chair. In my mind, every step of the transformation had been leading to this final crowning moment, but when Nick Arroyo, the hair stylist, took out his scissors, she put up her hand and said, "Stop right there. There is no way I am letting you cut my hair." Even though Nick pleaded and reasoned with her, she adamantly refused. Eventually she broke down into tears and said something I will never forget. She said, "My hair is *me!* If I let it go, I won't be me anymore. I can't be myself without it." Graciously, Nick gave in and did what he could to work around her restrictions.

What are you hanging onto that cuts the transformation process short in your life? Maybe you say things such as, "Italians are passionate, so of course I have a bad temper. That's just who I am," or "I was abused growing up, so of course I can't trust my husband." How about, "My parents were so legalistic and strict with me, I just can't discipline my child"? I determined a while back never to let my "No" be the thing that stops God's transformative process in my life. I know I have blind spots and, just like our friend, I can cling to the very things that are hurting me the most. I can get stubborn and refuse to let God do what He alone does best—make me over from the inside out.

We never need to fear that by fully offering ourselves to God we will experience any loss of our real selves. God is on our side and only has good intentions for us. He wants to bless us spiritually, emotionally, and physically beyond what we could ever imagine. But it does take willingness on our part to hold back nothing and to allow Him to completely deconstruct every part of our present identities. We cannot circumvent the reconstruction process, and our attitude must be, "Jesus, everything I have is yours; take every wrong belief and untrue value judgment, take my confidence in my own performance, take every dream and desire. Take all these things from me." It's only in that humility and honesty that we can begin to experience God's total reconstruction.

Thing #3

Everything is About to Change

There was nothing to do but wait. I had just taken the most intense bathroom break of my life. As I sat on the side of the bathtub, I gazed intently at the tiny windows in the pregnancy test I was holding in my hand. In the minute or so that passed, conflicting emotions bubbled inside me. On the one hand, feelings of excitement, joy, and in a weird way, relief surged through me. Stovall and I wanted a baby. We wanted to start a family, and now it could possibly be happening. On the other hand, I was scared. Yes, we wanted this, but maybe not exactly *right now*. We had only been married a little over a year, and I wanted more time just to be a wife. We made very little money. How could we support another human being?

The timer bell went off and jerked me out of my reverie back into reality. The line was pink. A tiny little line that didn't exist a few seconds ago was now staring me in the face confirming what I already suspected to be true. We were going to have our first baby! Ready or not, we had boarded the parenthood train with a one-way, non-refundable ticket and the estimated time of arrival to our final destination would be about 21 years in the future. There was no going back, and the prospect of what lay ahead of us was both thrilling and a little bit terrifying.

I knew that day would forever be burned into my memory as one of the major 'firsts' in our lives. A day when everything changed and life as we knew it ceased to exist. In truth, when I look back on that day from where I am now, I was absolutely right. It *was* a major first, and our lives *had* drastically changed. But I have to laugh at my former self holding that pregnancy test, because I had absolutely no clue what those words really meant. When I naively thought, *Wow! This is going to change everything.* I didn't truly understand that meant *everything...* as in, every... single...thing!

Our marriage changed. Our finances changed. My circle of friends changed. The way we managed our time changed. The way my body looked changed.). Date nights changed. Sex changed. Our conversations changed, changed, changed! There was literally no aspect of my life that wasn't altered by the arrival of our daughter. And while I generally believe change is a positive thing, I think I could have handled this complete life overhaul better had I been more mentally prepared for all it entailed.

Which brings me to the third thing I wish someone told me before I became a mom—Everything about your marriage is going to change, so Get Prepared!

But, how do you prepare for something when you have no idea exactly what it is you're supposed to be preparing for? You don't even know what questions to ask. And that is *precisely* why I'm writing this book. My desire is to offer you practical advice on many of the things I wish I'd have known when I first became a mom, so that hopefully you (and your husband) can be better prepared than I was.

For a couple entering into parenthood, much of this preparation is garnered through communication. Granted, much of parenting is a learn-as-you-go process, so it's impossible to talk out and forecast how you're going to respond to every possible future event. However there are many discussions that can happen beforehand to prepare you both for what lies ahead. Whether you are heading into, or are right in the midst of, this new season of life, this chapter deals with some of the biggest issues soon-to-be parents should cover, and actually prepare for, *before* the baby arrives.

Before we dive into these topics let me clarify one thing: men and women are not alike. (I know, BIG shocker!). We approach love and life from unique perspectives, so naturally we are going to communicate those perspectives differently. Having a baby is no different. Yes, it took two of you as a united front to create this baby, but sometimes how you handle the news and how you begin to execute your parenting plan is totally un-united. These differences aren't a bad thing; it's how God created us. But you *will* need to be ready to extend much grace for the variation. Every new parental unit must be ready to talk everything out, start to work it out, and then after a while, talk it out again!

**CAN'T YOU SEE SOMETHING IS DIFFERENT WITH
THIS PICTURE?**

From the moment I first saw the positive pregnancy test, the
fact that we were having our first baby began to sink into my
heart. How could it not? My body seemed to be taking on a life
of its own. I felt bloated, my breasts were sore, and then there
was that first trimester fatigue that hits you like an overloaded
barge. I wanted to nap 24/7!

Speaking of 24/7, I was obsessed. This baby was now all
I thought about. There was an actual precious being growing
inside me, and the awesomeness of this fact lingered in my
mind all day, every day. Will it be a boy or a girl? What will
she look like? What will he be like? What will we name
him? Is she forming just right? What part of her body is
being perfected today? I spent hours picking out cribs and
bedding, reading consumer reports of strollers and car seats,
and gathering resources on how to breastfeed. Everything
in both my internal and external worlds was merging in one
concentrated trajectory toward the arrival of our baby.

So why didn't Stovall seem to be feeling the same way?
Days would go by, and unless I brought the subject up myself,
he'd go on about his life as he always did, seemingly oblivious
to his child growing inside my womb. From the very beginning
it felt as though we were stepping into our new roles as parents
on two totally different planes. *Doesn't he fully comprehend the
gravity of this situation?* I often asked myself as I lay in bed at
night fighting nacho cravings.

As unbelievable as it might sound, ladies, the answer to
this question is "no." He does *not* comprehend the gravity of

the situation. But before we give into our frustration and start throwing our anti-nausea lollypops in his general direction, we need to give our guys a break. Remember, our husbands don't have the daily physical reminders—the fatigue, the nausea, the hourly trips to the bathroom—to keep them glued to the awareness that there is a new baby coming. In fact, in the Weems' household, it wasn't until my belly was pretty big and Stovall could actually feel the baby kick that the reality of my pregnancy began to sink in for him.

I had a choice to make during this time. I could be offended by Stovall's failure to resemble the sensitive, totally "into it" husbands on TLC's *A Baby Story*, or I could learn to grant him a grace period as he went on with his life, business as usual. He wasn't purposefully trying to be insensitive; he was simply unaware. Our baby had not become a reality in his heart. If this is your situation, don't worry. Your husband will get there and become head-over-heels obsessed with your little baby. It just might take a face-to-face meeting first.

WHAT DO YOU WANT LIFE TO LOOK LIKE?

As you both revel in the copious amounts of baby-free time you have at this point, I highly recommend having some brutally honest conversations about what you think your lives are going to look like once your baby arrives. You might find that you both have pictures of newborn parenting that are very similar. Or, you might be surprised to discover you each have very different views of what life-after-baby will look like. The only way to know is to spend the time asking each other questions *and* being super honest with your answers. Here are some vital ones to cover:

Are you both going to work after the baby is born?

This is a huge question that every couple must address. In fact, the next chapter will be entirely devoted to this subject, offering thoughts and wisdom about how to answer this question. I urge you to resolve this issue to the best of your ability long before the baby arrives; if possible, even before you both decide to get pregnant. The answer is crucial. It is the foundation for how you envision your life after baby. Take the time to really think this one through.

Are you ready to renegotiate your recreational time?

I believe this issue can become one of the biggest areas of contention between a husband and a wife. Before baby, you really do have more discretionary time. That's not to say you aren't busy, but it's busyness of a different kind. It's busyness in the areas that you choose to be busy in, the areas that hopefully return strength to you. Stovall and I lived busy lives.

Stovall is an avid outdoor sportsman and he loves to fish. And when I say fish, I don't mean he walks over to a nearby lake and throws out a hook to try and catch a catfish or two. Stovall is a *fisherman!* I knew this before I married him, and actually, I found his devotion to his hobby to be endearingly boyish. I loved that he pursued something with such passion. I used his time away with the guys to connect with my girlfriends. It was the perfect balance, when we were dating. It wasn't until after we were married and living under the same roof that I truly understood his dedication to the sport.

Here's how a typical week would go: On Tuesday after

work, he would start cleaning his boat for the weekend fishing trip and organizing the getaway with his buddies. *Where would they go? Who would go with them? What was the weather forecast?* Wednesday would be all about getting the proper bait and other supplies for the trip. Thursday was what I liked to call "hype day." Although there was no actual work to be done, there were numerous phone calls about the trip—talking up how much fun it's going to be and evaluating where the fish were biting according to fishing tales from friends who had been out in the last few days. The translation from my perspective? Time not spent with me. On Friday evening, he and his buddies would drive three hours to their favorite fishing spot, fish all night into Saturday, and pull in late Saturday evening. On Sunday, we'd go to church and take naps to catch up on sleep. Monday we'd both go to work and turn in early (him still wiped out from the weekend fish-a-thon). Come Tuesday, the cycle would start all over again. At least two or three weekends a month, Stovall lived out his rock-n-roll, *Deadliest Catch* fantasy.

Before we had kids, I completely supported this pastime. This was way before Stovall stepped into the role of Lead Pastor. We hadn't yet begun planting Celebration Church, so we spent plenty of time together in the margins of our days. The trips would refresh and invigorate Stovall, plus, as I said before, I'd have time to maintain and build relationships with my girlfriends whenever he was gone. We were loving life as DINKs (double income, no kids) and having a great time.

And then Baby Kaylan arrived.

For the first four to six weeks, Stovall stayed close to home as my body healed and we both settled in to a new schedule. I guess I just *assumed* he understood my needs and that he would probably forego any future fishing expeditions. Or at the very least, I thought he would go less often than he had in the past. Not so. After the six-week mark, one Tuesday evening, I noticed he was uncharacteristically late for dinner. I was wondering what could be keeping him, when I heard some suspicious clanking out in the garage. I poked my head out there to see what was going on, and was utterly shocked at what I saw. He was actually cleaning his boat! The evidence at the scene of the crime made his intent unmistakable—hooks lined up by size and type, bait organized by the fish they were meant to attract, tackle box out, new spools of fishing lines in varying tests, live bait well being cleaned and tested. He was getting ready to go on a fishing trip.

I didn't say much because I thought that since he'd been so great during the past weeks, he deserved to take off and enjoy a weekend with his buddies every once and awhile. Feeling utterly magnanimous, I congratulated him on his first trip since the baby, wished him a good time, went back inside and waited... alone. Finally, I ate dinner (still alone) while trying to nurse between bites. Slowly my magnanimous feeling began to wear off, and by the time he came in from the garage I was shooting nails at him out of my eyeballs. This was the first of many fishing-and-hunting-induced meltdowns that occurred during that first year of parenthood.

You see, the issue for me was that my life had completely changed ten months earlier when I peed on a stick and saw a little pink line show in up in that second window. That was way before Kaylan arrived. Now here she was—alive, breathing, and screaming—and he was *just catching on* to what that really meant.

Now, I would love to report to you how I somehow retracted the shooting nails, modeled the ideal wife, and tenderly talked with love and compassion about the renewal of his fishing addiction. I would like to say I supported his passion for the outdoors, yet ever so meekly reminded him of this new phase in our lives or that I suggested we could talk together about and strategize *ahead* of time for the ways we now would spend our recreational time. I wish I could tell you we had such a conversation and that it led to sublime marital bliss and family peace. Yeah, not so much.

My tirade went down something like this: "Why do you get to go back to your life as usual, having time to yourself, spending the weekend with your buddies, while I sit trapped at home like a milk tap on call, lonely and sleep-deprived, taking care of the needs of *your* baby, wondering when my next shower will be?!" My poor husband stared at me in disbelief, wondering who I was and what I had done with the real woman he married.

Truth be told, our issue was not the fishing trip; it was our lack of communication. We had never talked about our expectations of how we would balance our schedules after the baby came and how that would impact our recreational activities. In fact, we had never even thought about talking about it. We each just assumed the other would be happy to cave to the desires of the other. We were both completely exhausted by the level of time and energy a newborn demands.

Everything was brand new; we didn't know how to identify most of our needs and wants until we were in the midst of being needy and want-y. And that's *not* the best frame of mind for beginning a discussion.

We both recognized we needed to renegotiate how we spent ALL of our time, both together and apart. Stovall was very receptive once we were able to have honest and non-emotional conversation about our schedules. We both made the adjustments we needed to make, and the result was a much happier home and married life.

Here are some questions for you and your spouse to contemplate and discuss. I believe they can help you put some strategy toward how you will spend your free time (outside of work and other demands on our time). They can aid in getting some routine into your schedule beforehand and hopefully, help you chart a course for the new season ahead. Ask yourself and your partner:

- How do you think this new baby will change our schedule?
- Which hobbies/recreational activities are most important to you? Which ones could you give up, if necessary?
- How will we make sure to have date nights, with just the two of us?
- How much alone time do you require to feel refreshed?
- What are the relationships *outside of our marriage* we want to make sure we continue to build?

WHO'S GONNA DO WHAT?

The question of roles and responsibilities might seem
unnecessary and offensive, but let me assure you, this
conversation is essential. And it's a wise one to have pre-baby
so you both can address your expectations about gender roles.
This may sound a bit odd to bring up in our post-modern
21st century culture, but whether you are aware of it or not,
both of you have definite expectations. How you were raised
and the gender specific roles modeled in your home have
subconsciously created a blueprint in your mind. Not until you
share your experience in specific terms with your spouse will
you become aware of your differences. And remember, chances
are, you will probably have this conversation over and over
(and over and over and over) again.

Stovall came from a family where his mother did
everything related to the household. And I mean that literally.
She cooked, cleaned, did laundry (folded *and* put away), did
dishes, grocery shopped, cared for the children—anything that
had to do with the house in any remote way fell inside her
domain. Of course, Stovall took care of the outside things like
taking out the trash, washing the cars and keeping up the yard,
but the inside was his mom's job.

Can you imagine what our first years of marriage would
have been like had my mother taken care of everything for
me as well? Both of us would have been waiting for someone
else to get up and make dinner, and we probably would have
starved ourselves in the process! Luckily, we had this kind of
conversation prior to getting married and we quickly settled
into an arrangement well-suited for us.

But just because our systems were working at that moment, didn't mean that they would continue to work in every subsequent situation. This is true for all marriages, especially once babies enter the picture. As soon as a new family member comes onto the scene, all of those agreements need to be renegotiated and reconfigured. I only wish I would have known that the "Who's gonna do what?" conversation would have to be revisited after Kaylan was born, and again after Stovie was born, and *again* after Annabelle arrived. Why? Because the family dynamic shifts with the birth of each additional child. But no one had told me to expect it. So, as with the episode about the fishing trips, I just assumed life would automatically adjust. Well, we all know what happens when we assume.

Case in point: Three months after Stovie was born (Kaylan was three years old), Stovall asked me if we could host an "intimate" dinner for about forty of the leaders in our church. I love to host and plan parties, so I was totally game. It was Saturday morning, the day of the big event. I had all the food and little décor items purchased, and I would be spending the day cleaning the house and cooking the entire meal.

In a perfect world, my kids would have slept until noon, giving me the space for a head start on the day. That didn't happen. In a perfect world, Stovall would have woken up thinking about all the ways he could help me get everything ready for the dinner—*his* dinner—Yeah, that didn't happen, either.

But here's what *did* happen. The Weems (all of us) had been up for maybe a couple hours. I was multi-tasking my multi-tasking. I had a mop and bucket in one hand and a crying baby with a poopy diaper on my hip. A pot was boiling over on the stove and Kaylan had just walked into the kitchen with a box of sharpie markers and a guilty look on her face. Just then, my husband entered, showered and crisp-looking.

"Honey, do you mind if I go play a round of golf?" he asked.

In abject disbelief, I asked him to repeat himself. With all the commotion going on, I was sure I misheard him. He repeated himself, this time talk-shouting over all the crying.

Can you go and play a round of golf? I thought. *Are you kidding me? Are you living in the same house as me at this moment? Golf is the* last *thing on earth I want you to do right now. And I'm really offended that it even occurred to you as an option for today while I stay here alone, taking care of the kids and getting everything ready for* your *staff dinner tonight!*

That is what I wanted to say. And that is probably what I should have said (only nicer). But, in my harried state, I decided to put Stovall to the test. (I think at this point a fire alarm was going off somewhere in the house; I should have heeded its warning in more ways than one.) Instead of being honest, I said, "Sure, honey. You go and have fun with your friends." I wanted to see what he'd choose to do, if he really had the audacity to actually leave me in this pit of chaos and go live it up on the greens.

Guess what? He chose golf. But you know what? It was totally my fault. Rather than choosing to express my needs, I wanted Stovall to guess what they were. And although at the time it didn't seem like rocket science to figure out that playing golf was counter-productive to my sanity for that day, it was still incumbent upon *me* to make sure that my needs were expressed. Many times we find ourselves in situations where it seems as though our needs are being deliberately ignored. And who knows, maybe in some cases they are. But regardless of why it might be happening, when we see that our husbands just aren't getting it, it's time to speak up. We can't put the responsibility for our happiness on their shoulders. We are partners in this endeavor called parenting. We are on the same team, and the only way we can really win is by accepting responsibility for making our needs known through direct communication (*not* door slamming, eye rolling, or back-stabbing snide comments at a party).

Granted, a mature marriage relationship will, over the years, become keen to anticipate each other's needs. That's the wonderful fruit of cultivating your love for each other through a long span of time. But when this was happening, Stovall and I had been married less than five years. We had barely begun the "becoming one" process before we were pregnant with Kaylan, and Stovie came right on her heels.

Eleven years after that day, I look back and think, "What a stupid thing to do!" Had I simply taken the few moments necessary to calmly explain my needs to Stovall and named some things he could do to help me, he would have quickly changed his plans and made himself available for me. Instead, I set us both up for failure. I was mad at him all day and night. I was prickly as a cactus to our wonderful staff and leaders who gathered in our home that night, hiding behind tasks in the kitchen because I was so worked up over the unresolved golf conflict.

That night when Stovall and I climbed into bed, I was sending off major signals. You know the kind I'm talking about: It started with the sleeping apparel. In this case I chose my highest-necked, longest-sleeved, to-the-ground flannel nightie. Then it continued with sleeping position. I was so close to the edge of the bed that if he sneezed I would have tumbled to the floor. And we can't forget the pillow barrier. I set up a row of pillows between us so he couldn't accidentally touch me.

Eventually, of course, we worked it out and learned a huge lesson in the process: ASK the question! "Who is going to do what?" Don't assume you know his answers any more than he knows yours. Negotiating these details pre-marriage, then as newlyweds, then pre-baby, then post-baby, and then post-every-consecutive-baby will save you both a ton of resentment, unmet expectations, and heated arguments.

Here are some important questions to ask each other:

- Who is in charge of the housework? The cooking? The laundry?
- Who is responsible for the vehicles? The yard? The garage?
- Who does the errands? The grocery shopping?
- Who will manage the bills and monthly budget?
- When baby cries in the middle of the night, who gets up?
- Will you share in all of these? Some of these? None of these?
- Which of these, if any, are you willing to outsource?

LET'S TALK ABOUT TALKING

For most women, talking isn't a problem. Word counts and word quotas aren't the issues. However, quality vs. quantity can be an entirely different story. After children, there are so many more topics a couple must tackle, so many more emotional needs to understand, and so much less time available to cover them. We need to make sure our communication tools are sharpened. If you and your husband have never gone through any type of communication class, marriage communication seminar, or even read any with books on the topic, now is a great time to do it. During seasons of change, great communication can steer your marriage forward to new levels of success and intimacy. Conversely, poor communication can make very manageable challenges seem much bigger than they really are. This is why the #3 Thing is so important. We can prepare for the enormous changes parenthood brings by being great at simply talking things out. Then, when the crunchy moments of life happen, we already have some strategies in place to deal with them.

Yes, the #3 Thing I Wish Someone Would have Told Me Before I Became a Mom is that everything about marriage is going to change. And everything *did* change, but I must add that all that change was ultimately for the better. The main reason I can say that is because Stovall and I were determined to talk about important issues over and over again until we came to a place of understanding. Granted, the mutual understanding on some of these things took longer than I thought they would (some even took years), but we continued to work them out until we got there. You and your spouse can too.

Thing #4

To Work or Not to Work?

Something is seriously wrong with me, I thought. *How is it possible that I could feel so unsatisfied? I have an amazing husband, a beautiful six-month-old baby girl, and am fulfilling one of the highest Christian callings a woman can achieve, by being a mom. Why am I so restless, angry, and unsatisfied?* Sitting on the driveway curb outside my home, I was desperately trying to make sense of my world.

All the women who had gone before me had said how incredible motherhood would be and how precious and fleeting every single moment would seem. Once I became a mom, I'd discover realms of unconditional love I'd never thought possible and experience a deep satisfaction like never before. In addition, all my dreams for career and outside work would effortlessly be shelved for several years while I stayed home with my kids, helping them to grow up in the nurture and admonition of the Lord. As I remembered these women, they *were* fully living out those words; they were incredible moms, perfectly content and happy to manage every detail of motherhood and homemaking, nothing more and nothing less. So what in the world was wrong with me? Obviously, this was the next stage of my Christian life. Why couldn't I embrace it and be as settled and fulfilled as these women?

My thoughts continued down a slippery slope. *I'm a failure as a mom. I'm a failure as a wife. I'm a terrible example of what a Christian woman should be.* I knew I hit rock bottom when this thought passed through my brain. *Maybe that crazy Christian lady who landed on my doorstep while I was pregnant with Kaylan was right.* She had heard I was going to have my baby in the hospital, and since she firmly believed the scripture about a woman being saved in childbirth was literal, she had rushed right over. She tried to convince me if I birthed my baby any other way than the good Lord had intended (i.e. in my home, without any drugs) I could possibly lose my salvation. *Could it be that with every drip of epidural entering my body, my salvation dripped out of my spirit?*

KERRI, get a hold of yourself! My mind screamed (or was it the Holy Spirit?). I almost had to slap myself to regain a sense of reality. Certainly, none of those thoughts were true, as I had a firm understanding of God's love for me and my family. I knew He would never have led me on this path to confuse, frustrate, or hurt me. However, I could not deny that along with the joys of motherhood, I also had some pretty strong negative feelings about what was happening to me. I needed to find some answers.

So there I was, sitting on the curb outside my home as Kaylan napped, feeling miserable and defeated. I was very conflicted. On one hand, my heart was inextricably tied to my family and I certainly didn't want to neglect them, but on the other hand, I knew I had an identity beyond "wife and mommy." I loved the sense of achievement I felt at a job well done (and I am not referring to changing a poopy diaper in six seconds flat, although that is quite impressive), and I longed for the opportunity to express myself outside the context of my home. I knew I was at a crossroads. I could either wallow in my self-pity and probably end up ruining my life, or I could begin a pursuit for God-revelation. And, that is where we get the #4 Thing I wish Someone Had Told Me Before I Became a Mom: motherhood and work are not mutually exclusive. To take it one step further, being a great mom and performing with excellence in the workplace are also not mutually exclusive.

The focus of this chapter is on the practicalities of choosing whether or not to work after having children. Before we even embark, let's just acknowledge what we already know to be true. This is a sensitive issue as it resides at the very core of our identities and hearts as moms. We are wired to nurture and care for our families, and the very, very last place any woman wants to find herself in is making any decision that is to the detriment of her children. So it's in this passion that we pursue our journey of motherhood, wanting to find the perfect path of parenting. There's only one catch. Everyone's perfect path is different. How will you know which path is right, which one is wrong, and which one is specifically right or wrong for *you?*

For starters, remember that you are free in Christ to do what you are called and commissioned by Him to do, and you are free to do it without guilt. So for those of you who have the vision to stay home full-time and who are financially able to do it, awesome. Go for it and don't listen to anyone who tells you that you are not living up to your full potential or that you could be doing so much more with your life. Those statements are fuel for fear and discontent. They have no place in a life that is supposed to be fueled by faith. You are fulfilling the particular call of God for your life, and you will reap the reward of a job well done.

And those of you who believe God is keeping you in the workforce, move forward with freedom and wisdom. Be great at your job. Love what you do and don't listen to people who tell you that your children are going to grow up to be dysfunctional delinquents with abandonment issues because they were in a daycare. Again, those statements are full of fear and they cannot dwell together with faith. Remember our friend Wisdom from Chapter 1? She processes each and every decision from a posture of the fear of the Lord. If you stay in a place of reverence and submission to God, sensitive to the voice of the Holy Spirit, there is no doubt you will succeed. God will NOT let you stray into decisions and lifestyles that will harm your family.

One of the most freeing things I ever heard was in a message by Pastor Bobbie Houston, of Hillsong Church in Sydney, Australia. She said, "I truly believe it is impossible to follow God and yet lose what He has entrusted to you. Yes, of course, you can stuff it up through lack of wisdom, but if you follow Him you can be sure that He will never call you to do something that will cause you to compromise those things He has entrusted you with." Girls, God has entrusted many things to us as His daughters, and most important among them are our precious families. Don't you think that if God calls us to stay home full-time or go back to the workplace, He does so with a full understanding of the impact of that decision? We can trust him to preserve what He has entrusted to us as we step out in obedience to Him.

The reality is, moms on both sides of the court (stay at home and working) often feel they are playing for separate teams; one competing against the other to win MVP. In my opinion (and experience), the mommy wars are most furiously fought in the Christian world. It's funny how having scripture to back up our opinions can often make us act in a less Christ-like way. We become self-righteous. My hope is that as you read this chapter you will begin to see that first, *all* moms are working, full-throttle. They might work at home or in a career outside the home; but, wherever they are, you can be sure they ARE working. Secondly, I truly hope Christian women can catch up with the rest of planet and begin to see each other as sisters on the same team. We are not competitors. We are, as the famous *High School Musical* chorus says, "All in this together."

Unfortunately for me (and this might be true for you), I grew up in a Christian environment that only applauded the choice to stay home. All the teachings, books, and resources we had were geared toward the woman who put her career on hold to go for the higher calling of being in the home; it's just what the Christian woman did. Period. The end. To have any other value or desire in her heart was deemed selfish and not from God. Of course, if for some reason the mom *had* to work, well then, God would somehow give her the grace to hold down a job for as long as necessary, but as soon as she was able, she should return to her home.

Even today you'd be hard-pressed to find a large variety of Christian resources affirming and equipping women for being a mom *and* pursuing her desire to explore gifts and talents beyond that of motherhood. Why is that? I sometimes wonder if the Church has ignored addressing these women for fear that by doing so, they will validate this choice, giving it power. Then, God forbid, where would we all be? All the women might run amok outside their homes to pursue their dreams, neglecting their families. All the children will be left to fend for themselves. Obviously, I'm being facetious here, and yet I don't think I'm too far off from the truth about why the church has changed little in their message for the modern era. The last thing on earth we should be concerned about is the Christian woman neglecting her family. She would go down simultaneously changing poopy diapers, flipping pancakes, negotiating a time out, and ironing and scrubbing scummy bathtubs before she would intentionally neglect her family.

However, the fact is, 83% of women reenter the workforce within a year after having children.[2] And because the Church has not widely addressed this very prominent choice, Christian women who fall into this category are often ill-equipped for knowing how to find balance. I know; I was one of them.

A MOM IS A MOM IS A MOM
The first aspect I needed to address was my unique set of

core beliefs. (Remember, we talked about how integral our core beliefs are in Chapter 2.) As I did some soul searching, I realized one of my core beliefs was that once a woman had children, the best choice for her family was to put her career or ministry on hold in order to focus solely upon the needs of her husband and children. Even though caring for small kids was never a source of fulfillment for me (as a teen I avoided babysitting at all costs because I thought it to be so bor-r-r-ring), somewhere along the timeline of life, I had assumed this belief as a solid truth. I determined a woman could not effectively be her best for her family if she held down an outside job. When I married Stovall, we had both whole-heartedly agreed that when the season came for kids, I would stop whatever I was doing and become a stay-at-home mom.

The problem was, this was a very poor fit for me. I disliked so much of it—the repetitive nature of parenting tasks, the isolation, the never-ending diaper changes, the lack of tangible accomplishments, not to mention how it took all day to cook one meal because of the interruptions occurring every forty-five seconds. After only a few weeks of motherhood, I harbored feelings of resentment over my loss of freedom. I had feelings of jealousy toward all my other friends who were still childless and a veritable smorgasbord of negative emotions toward Stovall for... well, you name it and I felt it was his fault (even if it wasn't). And as for myself, I didn't like being around her much, either.

The only thing I knew to do was to draw near to God so He could help me make sense of it all. He showed me that while *intellectually* I held this core belief about motherhood, my heart believed something else. I was in complete conflict with who I thought I was supposed to be and who God truly wired me to be (there's that ID again). Much to my surprise, God was not asking me to try and squeeze awkwardly into the stereotype I had assumed was best for my life. Instead, He was leading me to readdress and change this core belief to fit comfortably into the calling He had designed specifically for me.

I asked God, *You mean, I can have my cake* and *eat it, too? I can satisfy my desire to work outside the home actually* and *still be a good Christian mother?* God's answer was surprising, You'll actually be a *better* mom if you embrace the Kerri I've created than trying to be someone you're not.

The weight of the world seemed to lift off my shoulders. And the funny thing was, once God helped me remove the limitations I had placed on myself, I realized my path really was not too far off course. I truly did want to be home with Kaylan, and certainly was not ready to give that up. I simply needed to think outside the box about how to be a great mom and wife effectively, as well as discover avenues to creatively express my other gifts and talents.

Obviously, my first objective was to discuss these new thoughts with Stovall. As my husband, he is the head of our household *and* my greatest ally; nothing would succeed if we were not in agreement. Also, as I mentioned earlier, we had both previously agreed once children were added to the Weems family, I would stay home and take care of them. I must admit I was a bit nervous to broach the subject because of the fear he would disagree and never support my desire to go back to work while Kaylan was still so young. I was right. Stovall did hold the core value that it was best for his wife to be the primary caregiver of his children, and with Kaylan less than one year old, he wasn't ready for me to look for a job outside the home. He strongly expressed his wish for me to be happy and fulfilled, but also his discomfort with placing our children in a daycare situation. I knew I needed to honor his convictions, but still try to find a creative compromise.

After quite a bit of research, I unearthed some exciting options. I've always loved to write, and I found several freelance options offering a win/win compromise. I could freelance my services as a writer and editor and complete all projects from home. Plus I'd have full control over my workload. By writing during naptimes, I'd be able to fulfill my desire for outside employment and still be fully available for Stovall and Kaylan. When I showed these options to Stovall, he was in complete agreement, and I immediately went to work (literally!).

In a matter of a few weeks, I was a completely different woman. I thrived on the outside social interaction my freelance work offered. I loved the challenge of finding new projects and completing them in my tight schedule; and, as a result, I also began to feel fulfilled in everything I was doing at home. Because I was happy and content, I became a much better mommy to Kaylan and much more attentive wife to Stovall (if you know what I mean).

I learned that, for many women, staying home and taking care of every detail of her children and home can be absolutely fulfilling. Others require additional challenge and expression to find the same amount of fulfillment. Both types of women are equally capable of being incredible wives and mothers. Neither one is more noble or more Christian than the other.

TO WORK OR NOT TO WORK?

So here is the $64,000 question: Do I go to an office or keep it at home? Countless arguments exist for both sides of this debate, and each family must sift through the specifics in order to find their best path. Here are some tips to help you decide.

1. Agreement is a Must. You and your husband must be in harmony about the issue of work; and this goes both ways. Sometimes the husband wants the wife to work and she does not, and sometimes the husband does not want the wife to work and she does. Because this is a book written by a woman, expressly for women, let me be candid. *Nothing* is worth discord in your home. The long-term well-being of your marriage and family is much more important that the short season of working or not working while your kids are in the home. Proverbs 14:1 says, "The wise woman builds her house, but the foolish pulls it down with her hands." (nkjv) Regardless of what your desire is, to buck against your husband or to try to force his hand in this major, lifestyle decision is not wise. Talk it through until you come to an agreement, and in the meantime come under the headship of your husband. If he happens to be wrong, God will honor your choice to honor your husband and will somehow bring your desires to pass. One thing we as wives must remember is that our husbands are NOT the enemy, no matter what *The View* or *Desperate Housewives* or your momma is trying to tell you. Our husband is a gift from God, and is actually our greatest ally and partner in destiny. You need him on your side.

2. Count the Cost. Make sure to carefully examine all the hidden costs of working outside the home while your children are young. Take a look at your net monthly paycheck and subtract your expenses such as childcare, after school programs, gas, food, clothes. Then decide if the difference is enough to offset the intangible costs of working including the stress of planning and packing for your children each day, the very limited time you now have to cook, clean, launder, and grocery shop, the emotional and physical fatigue you might be feeling, and the diminished amount of time you have with both your children and husband. Check your core beliefs and be diligent to be in alignment with them.

For some of you reading this book right now, you simply are so stir-crazy being at home with your kids, that you are looking for anything to give you a way out of the mommy madness. But making the choice to go back to work cannot be one made simply to stave off loneliness or to get a "Calgon-take-me-away" respite from the kids. You might only grow to regret your choice. Be honest with yourself about why you want to work outside the home. Many times, these emotions can be alleviated by proactively getting involved with groups like MOPS (Mothers of Pre-Schoolers) or by finding fulfillment in your church or community.

For most moms, work is not an option; it's a financial necessity. Be creative about ways to cut your costs. Job share with another person, and possibly even swap childcare with them. How much of your job can you accomplish from home? Perhaps you could propose a work-from-home plan to your boss and offer a time frame for you to prove your production capacity could remain the same. Perhaps you could cook extra meals on the weekends for another mom in exchange for childcare? Get creative, and remember to ask for help.

3. Plan Ahead. If you are pregnant, or plan to be soon, and you already know you will want to keep your present employment, work your tail off *now* to be utterly indispensable. No employer wants to lose excellent staff. If you prove yourself to be a self-motivated, highly competent employee before you become pregnant, you will have many more options at your disposal after your baby is born. Your boss will be more likely to work with you to meet your needs so he or she will be able to retain you (and your amazing productivity) once you are a mom.

You might be able to renegotiate your work hours. One lady I know works from 4am to 10am and her husband starts work at 10:30am. They need both incomes to survive, and this woman is willing to exert the discipline to make this schedule work. As a result, there is no childcare expense, and for this particular family, their plan is quite effective. This may or may not work for you. But strategize with your husband to find something that will *before* you are holding your precious baby in your arms.

4. Realize the "Drop-off" is difficult. Even in the best scenario along with the 100% assurance in your heart you are supposed to return to work, that first day (and subsequent days) dropping off your baby in childcare or leaving her with a sitter is going to be intense. As you stand there handing over the most precious part of your world to some other woman, you will suddenly become keenly aware of just how vulnerable and little he is. How will this caretaker know how to hold him the right way, or to decipher his many different cries, or how he needs to be burped at exactly a 47.5 degree angle? The urge to turn and run might be overwhelming.

Stop. Breathe. Remember the concrete decision you know you made to return to work. Breathe again. You can do it, although probably not without a few tears. This is NORMAL (even if you shed way more than a few tears). This day is not final, you can renegotiate your plan, and you can always change your mind; that's one thing women do best.

5. Put Systems in Place. Every working mom has much to juggle, and this is true for the mother who is fully engaged in the home, as well as the one who also decides to have additional employment. There is so much work to do— schedules for home-schooling or for kids going to schools, housework, shopping, errands, appointments, cleaning, the list never ends. I have found the only way to get it all done is to put systems, or organized plans, in place to accomplish these many tasks. For some, this means talking with your husband about hiring a cleaning service. It might mean saying 'no' to your child's desire to be involved with his fifth sport of the year or her twelfth dance class. Sometimes our schedules are simply too crazy and we just have to draw the line.

Maybe you organize carpools for before and after school. When I was a kid, my mom got creative with another mom of two children. My mom would take us and those kids to school early in the morning (giving that mom the freedom to sleep in a bit more because she only had her kids to get ready), and then my sister and I would go to that lady's house after school for an hour or so until my mom got off work. It was a definite win/ win for both moms. Don't be afraid to ask the mom right next to you; she's just as busy as you are and would probably love the help.

One of the systems I swear by is meal planning. I have a chart on my fridge where I plan every meal for my family for a two-week period. Not only does this save me money at the grocery store as I only buy the food I need for that meal plan, but it also saves me brain space. You'll never find me standing in front of an open refrigerator trying to remember what I fixed yesterday and what food I have left to create tonight's meal. It takes only a few minutes to plan and gives me way more freedom in my brain and my wallet. However you decide to approach it, some sort of system is a must.

Girls, motherhood and career are not mutually exclusive. Work. Don't work. Do a little bit of both. The most important thing for you to ask is what God has called you to do. If He has called you to serve and to minister inside your home, do that. If He has called you to be employed in some fashion, as well as serve in your home, then do that. You can hold the baby in one hand and the career in the other *if*, and only if, that is what is in God's plan. Proverbs 10:22 says, "The blessing of the Lord makes one rich, and He adds no sorrow with it." (NKJV) You can trust He will lead you in your role of motherhood, and wherever He takes you, you can rest assured that path will be blessed and will never be to the detriment of you, your marriage, or children.

Thing #5

Your Body Will
Never Be the Same

It was a day I had longed for my entire life and now it was here. It had finally happened. For the first time in my life, I could look at myself in a full-length mirror and smile with approval. Unbelievably, I liked what I saw. And, I'm not talking about of those magical, vertically-stretched illusions you get in department stores. You know, the type they hang all over the women's fitting rooms to trick you into buying every article of clothing you try on, including the swimsuits. I mean, I liked seeing my body in all mirrors and from *all angles*.

Because of this precious gift of self-esteem, I regularly thanked God for the mandatory P.E. classes I was required to complete in order to graduate with my college degree. Before I enrolled in them, I was like many young women. I hated my body. From the age of nine, I was the "chunky" one (no exaggerating, I have the cheesy grade school photos to prove it). By fourth grade, I was already putting myself on every kind of diet I could find, trying desperately to become the *un-chunky* one. Then throughout my teenage years, I was always trying to whittle down my body fat, and compensate for my height-challenged state. This simply became my way of life. I am now in my 40s with a maximum height of 5' 3," and that's only when I am standing up perfectly straight. I gave up on my dreams of being lean and leggy a long time ago.

But as a college student, I had learned about nutrition and the proper ways to work out my particular body type. I began to understand not only how metabolism and muscle to fat ratios work together, but also how to eat to maximize the benefits of both. For the first time in my life, I looked great and I felt great. I had NO body image hang-ups. That's right I said NONE, zero, zip, nada. I was completely emotionally and mentally free. It was a great feeling. I had worked so hard and so long, labored so diligently for this moment. I made a secret vow to myself that I would never, under any circumstances, *ever* go backward. This body was going to be the one I lived in for the rest of my life. When I walked into heaven the saints might need convincing that a glorified body was even necessary.

The End.

Except, not really.

Because this brings me to the #5 Thing I Wish Someone Had Told Me Before I Became a Mom: Your Body Will Never Be the Same. I must offer complete disclosure here. It's not that I *never* heard anybody say this before I had children. Probably most of us have heard this at some point. It's just that because of my denial, my response to this statement was, "Well, I'm going to be the exception to that rule. I'm going to work out harder and eat healthier than anybody in the history of the planet. I will be more ascetic than a Tibetan monk. By the sheer force of my will, I will defy the physiological impact of pregnancy." It was either that or, "Fine. I just won't have any babies."

Deep down, I knew these responses were unrealistic, but I had to at least try to convince myself of their possibility. My fear of losing my present body was so great that trading it in for a baby seemed to be too big of a sacrifice. Any woman who has struggled with her body image (and if statistics are any indicator, I'm guessing that would be the majority of us) can grasp why this could be a hurdle. From the time we are little girls, most of us experience at least some kind of dissatisfaction over our appearance. It is a well-known fact that even the most beautiful women stress out from time to time over the little flaws that only they see. So where does that leave the rest of us "everyday beauties"?

The problem with my newfound freedom was that it wasn't actually freedom. Not in the true sense, anyway, because soon after Stovall and I got married, the fear of what pregnancy would do to my body became a huge issue for me. I knew the day was coming when we would decide to have babies. And the truth was, I *did* want to be a mother. I wanted kids, a bustling, happy family and everything they would add to my life. I just wished there was some alternative to having to actually birth them from my own body. I secretly thought that it would have been much kinder of God to arrange for us to go about this processes with less physical impact. What if, like birds, we could somehow lay a nice tidy little egg and look on lovingly as it grew (huge) and developed *outside our bodies.* Of course, my only reason for even thinking these ridiculous thoughts was complete, unbridled insecurity with a (un)healthy dose of vanity mixed in.

So with that in mind, I think it would be more accurate to rename this chapter "Your Body Will Never Be the Same After Pregnancy... and It's *Okay.*" It's that second part—the "It's *Okay"* part—that's vital. *And* it's also the part I rarely heard women talking about. I got full disclosure on the bodily sacrifices of birthing children. I heard earfuls of the complaints about stretch marks, sagging in strategic places, crepe-y bellies. But to hear women celebrating what their bodies looked like post-pregnancy? Now that was rare. I hardly ever heard another woman confidently talk about how, although her body is different, she still loves the way she looks. No one seemed to be talking about how to embrace and be at peace with their new "womanly physique," which by the way, means the saggy, new mama shape that can say goodbye to wearing low-rise jeans without the help of Spanx.

Maybe you can relate to my experience. I have a hunch I'm not the only one who has ever waded through the mire of a crummy body image. So whether you are pre-prego, post-prego or presently prego, hopefully this chapter will help you sort through these very real fears, feelings, and disappointments about how your body will change or has changed, since giving birth. Let me assure you, after having three children of my own, I most definitely do not cruise around in the same body I had before babies (remember, I am only 5' 3", and I had really big, babies). However, I can honestly say that I have come to terms with my reality. I have learned to love my self every bit as much as I did when I was in college, and I have the eternal blessings of children to boot.No,, your body will never be the same again... but it is *okay*.

PRE-PREGO

Let me share with you a life lesson that spans far beyond the season of pregnancy and motherhood. As women, we like to feel secure. In a utopian world, we'd have everything perfectly planned and figured out for today, for tomorrow, and for the rest of our lives. But the truth is, as we all know, this will never be the case. Life happens. Change happens. Difficult times happen. Most of our days are going to be "make-it-up-as-we-go-along" days, rather than "every-moment-is-going-perfectly-as-planned".

The same thing is true emotionally. We want to be completely certain we are making the right decision before we move forward. We want to process our feelings about things from every possible angle. We want emotional security. The problem with that is when we are thinking about our futures, there is simply no way for us to be fully, 100% prepared. How is it possible to thoroughly prepare ourselves mentally and emotionally for something we have never before experienced? In addition, if we wait until we have our thoughts and feelings all sorted out before we step into a new season, we will never step out because we will never achieve that level of surety.

Before I became pregnant with our first child, I was scared about losing my figure. It just didn't seem worth it. What if Stovall didn't find me attractive anymore? And what am I going to have to sacrifice to get my body back? Is having a baby worth never eating dessert again? From outside the experience of motherhood, everything about it seemed overwhelming. The whole body-image thing was the straw that broke the camel's back. As I talked with God about this huge thing called motherhood, He began to speak to my heart and to help me understand what it means to walk by faith.

Whenever God asks us to step out into a new realm of life, a new project or a greater challenge, the situation almost always seems too big for us, doesn't it? It's scary. It fights against our innate craving for security, and we can find ourselves caught in a whirlwind of doubt. But as soon as we take even a small step of faith toward God's plan for our lives, His grace *always* meets us there. In this instance, I was attempting to mentally and emotionally conquer motherhood before I actually stepped into it. I wanted to be uncompromisingly confident that I would be able to handle the responsibility once I actually entered into this role. But faith doesn't work that way. We step forward first, and then God's grace envelops us and gives us the strength and ability to walk it out. Our challenges appear remarkably *less challenging* when we view them from the vantage point of empowering grace.

In essence, if you are struggling with your fears and insecurities about what will happen to your body once you start having babies, you will never find peace in your heart and mind about it until you simply make a decision and take a step of faith. , Yes, the unknown is scary. Yes, your body is going to go through tremendous change. No, it will never look exactly the same again. But, it's okay. You *will* be able to lose your baby weight, or at least most of it, if you are diligent. And you *can* learn to love your new body unconditionally if you put your heart and mind into it.

In the meantime, here are some simple and doable tips to help you prepare your body for pregnancy. The more you prepare ahead of time, the easier (and faster) you will be able to fit into your jeans again (the ones without the elastic panel in the front.).

1. Work Out Now. Go into pregnancy as fit as possible and you will be rewarded later. Our muscles have a sort of memory, called muscle memory, which helps them go back to whatever state they were in prior to pregnancy a bit more quickly and easily. If your muscles were strong and in shape, then when you start working out again after the baby arrives, they will quickly 'remember' what they once were. They'll lift and shape back up much faster for you than for the mom who waited until she was finished having babies to begin an exercise routine. Even simply learning how to stretch all the muscles in your body will do wonders. Remember all those stretches you had to do during high school P.E.? All of those actually work. They're easy to do and you already know how to do them.

2. Learn about Nutrition. There is so much information at our fingertips these days; use it to your advantage. Inform yourself. Find out what foods are good for your body pre- and post- pregnancy. We can all attest to the fact that it's not only pregnant women who get intense cravings. (Pre-menstrual chocolate cheesecake binge anyone?) Let me promise you that your second or third trimester is not the ideal time to begin to deal with food cravings. Start now. And while you are sure to give in sometimes (be kind to yourself when you do) you will be much better equipped to deal with cravings during pregnancy. And as for liquids, you can almost never drink too much water. A hydrated body is a happy and clean body. Plus water can offset any adverse effects from caffeine. Many coffee-holics—and I'm talking about myself, here—find it impossible to completely eliminate this heavenly nectar from our diets. If you can work on breaking your attachment to caffeine it will make a big difference down the road. If you must have it, water will help minimize the impact. Here's another bonus with getting into the habit of drinking water. When you are hydrated, you can experience less nausea during those first few months of pregnancy.

3. Build Support. Talk with your husband about how important it is for you to stay in shape during and after the pregnancy. It will be to his advantage as well as yours, so prepare him for the expectation of helping while you go to the gym a few times a week. It will be really discouraging to get dressed to work out, pack a diaper back, go to the gym, drop the baby in the gym nursery (all the while dealing with a little separation anxiety), and get into the good, sweaty part of your cardio, only to be called back to the nursery because the baby can't stop crying. Let's be honest. If working out is a challenge for you before you have kids, it will take an act of God to get you to the gym afterward. You will need your husband's help, so just ask for it. He would much rather watch the kids for two hours while you work out than listen to you complain about how fat you are every day of the week.

PRESENTLY PREGO

Perhaps you are already pregnant and just now reading this book. You're thinking, *Uhh, yeah... I didn't get the memo about making sure I was fit* before *I got pregnant, so now what do I do?* No worries. There is still hope. Before Stovall and I started dating, I was working out every day, sometimes twice a day (obsessive, I know). A few months into our dating relationship, those late nights on the phone made it harder and harder to wake up at 5 a.m. and head to the gym. A few more months later, and I went from working out six times a week to four. By the first few months of our marriage, dinners out after work had altogether replaced my afternoon workouts, not a good trade off when it comes to weight management. I gained about ten pounds by our first anniversary. Clearly, I rode on the coattails of how incredible I looked in my wedding dress a little too long. But Stovall and I were having so much fun together, I conveniently forgot to keep up my workout regimen and the pounds crept on.

While I never lost those ten pounds before I became pregnant with our first baby, everything turned out fine. I made sure to be careful about what I ate, and kept my weight gain inside the range my doctor suggested. There are many books available about how to keep control your weight while pregnant, but here are the suggestions I'd offer to every pregnant woman:

1. Grace, grace and more grace! You must give yourself a large margin of grace. Your body, emotions, and life are going through some of the most significant changes you will ever face. Don't expect perfection. In truth, there is no bull's eye of perfection when it comes to pregnancy anyway, so if this is what you are shooting for, it's a moving target. Some days you will eat great, feel great, and even fit in some exercise; celebrate these days. And some days, you will give in to cravings and barely get off the couch; give yourself the needed grace and make a decision to try harder tomorrow.

2. Monitor baby's growth... and yours! Try your best to stay within the range of weight gain your doctor recommends. This can be difficult from week to week. Some weeks the baby isn't growing quickly, and other weeks, he is developing by leaps and bounds. Becoming aware of the growth patterns of developing babies will help you understand stagnant weigh-ins as well as sudden spikes on the scale. Also, this knowledge will deter you from casually eating anything and everything just because your weight didn't grow this month.

3. Moderation, Moderation. There is a difference between baby pounds and Cheeto pounds. Just because you're prego, you don't have a get-out-of-cellulite-free card! As your belly grows, there will be days when you want to just give up and pig out on ice cream, donuts, and Cheetos. Resist! It's okay to give into your cravings every now and then, but weekly pig-outs could result in a fat baby (which is more difficult to deliver) and a whole lot more weight to lose after your chubby-chubs is born.

4. Do something. Move. Walk up your stairs. Don't just sit in front of the TV. Do sit-ups or stretches while watching your favorite program. Just do *something!* Even in your last weeks, try to keep yourself mobile. Every little bit helps. Remember, every time you go anywhere you are essentially lugging around a 25-lb sack of potatoes, so almost anything you do can count as a mini-workout.

POST-PREGO AND BEYOND

I'll never forget the day I happened to catch a glimpse of my entire body in the mirror after my first daughter, Kaylan, was born. A few months had passed, and I was lucky enough to have already dropped most of my baby weight. I was feeling really good about being able to squeeze into my pre-pregnancy jeans, but I don't think I had yet to take an honest and thorough look at myself in a full-length mirror.

This was one of those drive-by sightings when you're scurrying to the shower. You think you just saw someone else moving in the room, you quickly turn to confront the intruder only to see yourself in the mirror. This was a brutally honest moment for me. I had surprised myself *with* myself, so I hadn't taken the time to make sure I was standing perfectly straight, shoulders back, tummy sucked in, and up on my tiptoes to produce a few extra inches. It was the real me in all my glory.

Whoa, I thought. *The number on the scale might be the same, but I sure don't look the same!*

I'm not going to lie to you; I was a bit disappointed. But only a little, because I knew I still looked great for just having a baby, and I was confident in a few more months, I'd be back to my normal self. I was able to take this moment in stride. And I think I handled the body changes fairly well until after our third baby was born. This was an entirely different situation.

Stovall was manning all three kids on this particular evening so I could go upstairs and take some time for myself. I drew a wonderful, hot aroma-therapeutic bath, lit some scented candles, turned on my favorite music, and sank into the tub. It was blissful. I closed my eyes and, for a long time, soaked in this heavenly atmosphere.

Then, I accidentally looked down at what I thought was my bellybutton. *What is this?!* Upon closer examination, I was forced to face a startling truth. I now had a communion cup for a bellybutton! You know those little plastic communion cups we pass down the rows at church? Yeah. That's pretty much was I was looking at. *Where did my other, small, adorable bellybutton go?! All I'd need is a straw and I could drink grape juice outta this thing! Really? Is* this *where we're gonna land after having three babies? A communion cup for a bellybutton?*

My tranquil bath had suddenly turned into a serious come-to-Jesus meeting about my new mama body. And this was where the true internal work for me began. All those scriptures about youth fleeting, about wisdom being the most valuable possession, about beauty not being about outward things, but inward qualities, began to rise up in my heart. I knew I had to make a decision about what I was going to accept as my truth.

First, I allowed myself to be honest. In truth, I did grieve the passing of my youthful and perky body. I had worked so hard, and although I was now at a very good weight for my body, I was never going to look exactly as I did in college. I had a communion cup for a bellybutton, and that was that. It was time to make peace with it, no matter how strong the urge to live the rest of my life draped in oversized shirts and stretchy pants. I decided I was going to renew my mind, to embrace my reality, and learn to love my body, all 5' 3" of it.

Don't ever forget the important part of the reality of a different-looking body after pregnancy—it's okay. The emotional journey to okay is different for every woman. But if we are to have true freedom and peace with ourselves, it's a journey we all need to take.

As I mentioned earlier, I was completely opposed to the notion of trading in my fit body for a post-pregnancy one. I believed I had finally come to a place of true freedom with my body-image and I was not ready to give that up. The problem was, the freedom I and peace I felt was neither true freedom nor *true* peace. You see, all of the peace I had made with myself was because I had finally arrived as close as humanly possible to the type of beauty that I held in my heart as ideal. My security in this area was still completely based on what was on the outside. And as much as I might wish to stop time and a stay perfectly fit, proportioned, and perky for the rest of my days, there is no denying that with or without pregnancy, we are all aging. One way or another, our bodies are going to sag, droop, and eventually stop altogether. I could do it pre –

mid - or post pregnancy, but one day I would have to come to terms with this truth: "Charm is deceptive, and beauty does not last; but a woman who fears the Lord will be greatly praised" (Proverbs 31:20, NLT).

It kind of blows my mind that several *millennia* ago God took care to address one of the most enduring existential struggles that women throughout the ages and from every culture have faced—our beauty. We often wrestle to see the beauty in ourselves. Instead, we envy the beauty of others and spend loads of time and energy trying to achieve an elusive ideal. But as Proverbs tells us, we don't keep our looks. Outward beauty is destined to fade. Now don't get me wrong. I encourage doing the best you can with what you have been given, but the outcome of our struggle with aging is already known; we lose. As George Bernard Shaw so eloquently put it, "Death is the ultimate statistic. One out of one people will die." And only in the resurrection will we see life that never fades and beauty, pure beauty, as it was meant to be seen. It is this kind of eternal, inward beauty that we should strive for, fight for, here and now.

But in the meantime, we will need to live out our time here—and the inevitability of sagginess it brings—with an attitude of grace and confidence. For me, this meant learning how to maximize all the earthly resources that are currently available. There are some very practical things I've done to embrace my body and work with it rather than fighting against it. Let me share what I've learned.

1. Learn how to dress your body shape. For some this comes naturally, while for others, you might need to enlist a close friend to help. And when in doubt, there's always *What Not To Wear.*

Be honest with how you look *today* and learn how to accentuate your best features. Most people who look awkward in their clothes are either buying clothes for the body they used to have or wish they had. What they don't realize is that if they would simply learn what styles work best for their unique shape, they could still be fashionable and look gorgeous.

I am shorter with an hourglass figure, so I have learned work with what I have rather than against it. For instance, I rarely leave the house without some semblance of a heeled shoe because it makes me look taller and more slender. Couple that with full-length jeans or pants (meaning to the floor with my heels on), and I look like a supermodel (okay not quite, but almost.). No capri pants or blocky, unbelted shirts for this girl or I start to look like a walking rectangle. Simple tricks like these can help boost your body image and help you feel beautiful.

2. Pay Attention to Your Make-Up, Hair, and Nails. A kept hairstyle, manicured hands, and a touch of make-up can go a long way to helping you love your appearance. If you are always throwing your hair back in a ponytail and running around without make-up, you will probably feel frumpy and undone. These practices don't have to be expensive. You don't have to go to the nail salon and get a professional mani-pedi or get expensive highlights and hair processing. It's about maintenance you can do at home with an emery board, cuticle remover, and the right boxed hair color. Granted, if you are a natural-beauty type of a gal, definitely embrace who you are; but, if you're just being lackadaisical, I urge you to take the time to take care of yourself. Pampering yourself—whatever this means to you—is one way of learning how to value all you have to offer and expressing that love to yourself.

3. Discover the Benefits and Pleasure of Exercise. Ladies, there is just no way around it, you must exercise your body. This isn't just for the goal of being "thin" or fitting into a certain size. It should be simply because you have a desire to live a long, healthy life. Your body will naturally respond, plus, your heart will be strong, your muscles will stay supple, and your mental health will remain positive. You will be amazed at how much better and more capable you feel. As I said earlier in this chapter... do *something!* Get up and move, your whole body will thank you for it.

SEX

Yes, I'm going there. I've dedicated the entire ninth chapter to the topic, but will touch on it here. This is a huge issue that many women don't want to address honestly, especially with regard to the way our bodies look. As we discussed in Chapter 3, just as with everything else in marriage, your sex life will also change after babies are thrown in the mix. But change, by all means, doesn't need to be a bad thing. And having a positive body image is vital to maintaining a fun, carefree sex life.

The first truth we must understand is that you are way more

worried about how your body looks than your husband is. Unless you have gained an enormous amount of weight since you were married, most husbands honestly don't obsess like we do about the body changes that inevitably occur over time. While you are checking out your naked body in the mirror, scrutinizing every inch trying to find if you've accumulated any more cellulite dimples, he's checking you out, wishing you'd dive your dimpled self into the bed. All he cares about is that you are happy and feel comfortable enough to have unabashed sex with him. He doesn't want to hear you always picking out the flaws of your body and complaining about how you wish you looked like someone else. His desire is for you to be confident and to see yourself as the beautiful woman he believes you to be.

If you are battling your self-image, talk with him about your feelings. Allow him to be a part of the process, and hopefully, a part of your healing. Maybe you both could set some tangible goals that will help you move forward in this area. But remember, you are his wife, his best friend, and the mother of his children. You are so much more to him than a perfect body, and if you give him the chance to express it, you'll begin to believe it.

There is no stopping time. It's moving forward, and will continue to do so until earth life, as we know it, ceases to exist. Likewise, our bodies are moving forward (or maybe it's more accurate to say, heading south!) and the years are going to take their toll on our bodies. We can fight it, we can dye it, we can lather cream on it, and we can nip and tuck it, but inevitably we are going to feel the effects of age. Let's resolve not to chase after the wind by continuing to mourn the loss of our physical youth. Rather, let's embrace each passing day *and* determine to lift our vision to gain an eternal perspective as we grow in maturity with God.

2 Corinthians 4:16-18 tells us,

Therefore we do not lose heart. Though outwardly we are wasting away, yet inwardly we are being renewed day by day. For our light and momentary troubles are achieving for us an eternal glory that far outweighs them all. So we **fix our eyes not on what is seen, but on what is unseen,** *since what is seen is temporary, but* **what is unseen is eternal.** (NIV, emphasis mine)

Yes, it's true our outward person is perishing day-by-day, and it would be silly to pretend there isn't a certain sadness that accompanies that realization. But our inner spirits are being renewed by the Holy Spirit day-by-day. As this mortal coil grows fainter, the glory of the spirit in us grows brighter and brighter leaning into that day when we will see God face to face! (I Corinthians 13:12) Our job in this earth-life is to follow the leading of the Spirit toward life and peace (Romans 8:6).

Let's celebrate that and value what God values.

Thing #6

Learn to Live Life in the Margins

To every new mom, there is one word that becomes more glorious than all others. It's a word, completely unremarkable to many before motherhood, but afterward, its worth cannot begin to be measured. Its power is far-reaching, and the mere sound of it can evoke myriad unique responses. To one mom, it brings a rush of adrenaline to conquer her world, to another an overwhelming sense of relief and well being, and to yet another, a joy unspeakable. The word is none other than... NAPTIME!

Before having Kaylan, my understanding of the word was one-dimensional, because being the driven young woman I was, I never saw the value of the concept. Naps are for wimps, for people who didn't have anything better to do with their time, right? After all, who in their right mind would ever want to press pause for a few hours—in the middle of the day, no less—on this exciting thing called life? What a complete waste of time. Little did I know then, that in a few short years, every one of my days would be completely structured around and controlled by this novelty called naptime.

In the immediate days after our first baby arrived, I began to understand another dimension of the word. Naptime was a no-brainer. "When the baby sleeps, you sleep," the doctor had ordered. It was the best prescription for my body to heal, for my milk to come in strong, and for my post-partum recovery to be complete. But after those short weeks were over, I think I thought my pace of life would just kind of go back to normal, only I'd have an added accessory (a.k.a. Kaylan). Sure there'd be the scheduled feedings and diaper changes, but then I'd be able to hoist her on my hip, kind of like a cute over-sized purse, and accomplish everything I needed to throughout the day.

Wow. I couldn't have been more wrong.

It didn't take long at all for me to conclude that this addition to the family seemed to have caused my time to Shrinky-Dink down to a tiny pocket-sized portion. Have you ever made those crafts? You color the picture of the pony on the special Shrinky-Dink paper, cut it out, and then bake it on a cookie sheet in the oven. Before you put it in, the pony is three inches wide but after baking, it becomes a thicker, wavy, and much smaller picture of its former self.

In essence, that's what happened to my time. Before baby, I seemed to have plenty of space in my day to finish my To Do list—the household tasks, the grocery shopping, and my work. After baby, my time seemed to shrink up into a hot, wrinkly, miniature mess. Yes, I had the same twenty-four hours, but it was most definitely a *much* smaller image of its former self.

I began to understand the inestimable value of naptime, and not just for the baby to sleep, or catching up on my own, much needed rest. Naptimes became the glorious two-hour space that still belonged to me. And it was in this space that I needed to accomplish nearly *everything* on my agenda! When baby slept, I slept *and* cooked *and* cleaned *and* completed writing assignments *and* reconnected with friends *and* did laundry *and* worked out. *And, and, and.*

This brings us to the #6 Thing I Wish Someone Told Me Before Becoming a Mom: Learn to Live Life in the Margins. By this, I am referring to margins of time. If you want to transition smoothly into the pace of motherhood and all it entails *with* your sanity intact, you must become adept at scheduling life in the margins of your time. And for me, along with countless other moms across the globe, those margins of time became synonymous with naptime.

WE HAVE THE MARGIN, WE JUST DON'T KNOW IT

We've all seen the circus-juggling act. The guy starts with three balls and begins to expertly circle them around. Then someone throws in a fourth ball, a fifth ball, a sixth ball, a seventh ball and the clown continues to juggle with ease. The speed with which the balls orbit is faster, but he has practiced this act for years and rarely drops one.

Metaphorically, this is how many of us handle our time before having children. The balls are all of our activities, responsibilities, and hobbies. For years, we've learned how to manage all of our balls, how to accomplish all we need to in the allotted twenty-four hours we all have been given. We have a routine, we move faster some days and slower on others, but we pretty much are able to keep all the balls in flight. This definitely represented me before motherhood. But after Kaylan came, it seemed as though not only was I unable to keep the usual balls going, but also that life was constantly surprising me by randomly beaming new balls at me (with quite the velocity, I must add).

Before baby, the juggling game was a fun game—the more objects, the more speed, the better. Bring it on! But now, I was starting to feel out of control. It seemed that my capacity had been reduced exponentially, and that I was now spending my days in a reactionary mode of sorts, merely trying to survive as I attempted to keep track of all the balls of life. I was living in a frenzy, just trying to keep up, frustrated most of the time and exhausted all the time. I convinced myself that I just didn't have enough time in my day to accomplish all that was needed, and that I might as well just give up trying to live a sane life. It was in this defeated place where God began to speak to my heart and show me the truth of my reality.

The truth was, I had the time. I just didn't know or see it. God has given every human being the same amount of time in a day. It's been said that time is the "Great Leveler," and I believe it. From the poorest to the richest person on the planet, from the meekest to the most powerful and influential, twenty-four hours is what each person gets.

My problem wasn't a lack of time. My problem was I didn't know how to use it and manage it anymore. The systems that had worked for me before were simply not going to work in this new phase called Motherhood. While there were activities I could accomplish with Kaylan strapped to my body or playing in the baby swing, there were many that required my single focus to really finish appropriately (i.e. working out, writing at my computer, taking a shower, and daily devotions, to name a few). I knew I needed to restructure how I used my time, reevaluate my priorities, and *intentionally* strategize how I was going to use each minute of each day only. I could do this knowing:

- Where my margins of time were;
- How many margins I would have; and
- How to properly fill those margins with only what they could handle.

For me, "margin" essentially meant Kaylan's naptimes. In those first twelve months, I had two naptimes a day, each taking two hours. During these nonconsecutive blocks of time, I needed to accomplish everything that could not be done with my lovely daughter in tow. Now, depending on how you structure your home and life as a mother—to work or not work, to be at home, or to use childcare in or outside the home— your margins might be different. Your margins might happen later in the evenings, on the weekends, or early in the morning if you're an early riser (which I am NOT by any stretch!). Whatever the case may be and whether or not you can see it right now, the margin is there. You just need to learn how to find it.

A YES IS NEVER JUST A YES

In her book, *Can I Have and Do it All, Please,* my friend
Christine Caine teaches women that we *can* have and do it all
in life; we just can't have and do it all at the same time. This
statement couldn't be truer. Once I became a mom, I gained
this personal revelation. Remember the ball illustration? Before
Kaylan, I had all my juggling balls in perfect rotation: friends,
marriage, ministry, career, and recreational time. I thought the
motherhood ball would simply be tossed into the rotation of
the others. What I hadn't accounted for was the fact that the
motherhood ball was so much larger than all the others. It was
like adding a ginormous beach ball into a slew of tennis balls.

Everything about my juggling act needed to be revamped;
and, in the process, some of those other balls needed to be set
aside for the time being. As I began to examine my priorities
and the elements of my schedule that really meant the most to
me, I learned that saying yes to something is never *just* saying
yes. It also means saying no to something else. For instance, in
Chapter 4, I talked about how I discovered I wasn't wired to be
at home with my babies and to completely discontinue working
on career projects.

In saying yes to writing projects, however, I also had to
say no to some other things. I only had small windows of
productivity each day to accomplish my goals. So if I had a
project deadline to complete, a house to clean and a friend who
wanted to come over and visit, that was one too many things
to fit into my available time. I had to choose which two were
priorities for that particular day and make some sacrifices.
If I wanted to work out, spend relaxing time reading, *and*

do laundry while organizing my closets, again that was one too many tasks to fit into my daily margin. Do you see how intentional I had to become? I had to be very deliberate about sorting out what I needed to do and what I wanted to do and choose wisely based on the time available.

Granted, not every single day had a rigid game plan, but for the most part I learned that if I chose to intentionally, rather than vaguely, or haphazardly, utilize the margins of time I had available, I was a much happier mommy, wife and friend. Instead of feeling overwhelmed, out of control and frustrated all the time, I began to embrace this season with newfound confidence and fulfillment. And whenever I sensed the life-is-darting-those-balls-at-me feeling again, I would take time to reevaluate what my yes's were, and what my no's needed to be.

If you are reading this and thinking, "Well, I'm not sure I want to say no to anything I'm doing right now," let me encourage you. First of all, no season of life lasts forever, that's why they're called "seasons." The desires you hold dear in your heart were actually placed there by God so He could have the pleasure of fulfilling them. He will not let you down. If there are some aspects of your life that need to be set aside for a time, you can trust in God to bring that desire back to you in your lifetime. And second, no amount of money, success, fame or adventure will be able to satisfy your heart if your home is chaotic or if your kids aren't living happy lives. There's a saying, "You're only as happy as your least happy child." Trust me, this is a truth! You will never, ever regret temporarily saying no to a few opportunities in your life and saying yes to being the best mom you can be.

MARGIN STRATEGIES

As I walked through that first year with Kaylan, then the subsequent births of Stovie and Annabelle, I learned a few invaluable strategies to living life in the margins. I hope these three main strategies will help you as you enter into this amazing season.

1. Simplify. Telling a 21st century woman who is about to become a mom that she is in need of simplifying her life can seem oxymoronic, even absurd. Because in today's society, so many of us are entering into motherhood as we are concurrently building our marriages and our careers. Simplification is the farthest thing from our minds. But take it from me, it most definitely is necessary, and with a carefully devised plan of attack it is possible.

Here are a few questions to ask yourself about how you spend your time. Your answers will help you understand what your priorities are and what you value. When the time comes to weed items out of your day-planners, these thoughts will help clarify your process of simplification.

1. What parts of your schedule are essential for you?
2. Is there anything you are doing simply because you've always done it? This could include activities that are recreational, relational, or service-related.
3. Are there areas in which you spend time because someone else pressures you, or because you'll feel guilty if you don't?
4. What activities or habits strengthen and recharge you? Are you making room for these?

5. What activities do you just love to do?

6. Are there time management systems that used to work, but aren't the best for this new season of life?

7. What activities are just mindless time-wasters? Can these be eliminated?

8. Are you holding on to some activities simply because they feed your ego even though they stress you out?

9. Are there any charitable activities or causes you are supporting that you can set aside for a time when you have fewer demands?

Once you've pondered these questions and given yourself some truthful answers, reevaluate your priorities. Allow your answers to offer you a window into yourself and to help you recognize what areas are most important and life-giving to you. Then prepare yourself for the possible pruning and purging of the things that are expendable.

2. Childcare. You are going to need to take a break. There's just no way around it, so I'm not even going to attempt to package it fancier. You are going to need to take a break. And this means without the baby. And without the husband. Just you doing something you like to do.

A pivotal moment for me in the early years of motherhood was the day I made it okay not only for me to want to take a break, but also for me to follow through and actually do it. I was reading a book by James Dobson, American psychologist, Christian author, and founder of *Focus on the Family.* He stressed the importance for mothers, especially mothers from birth to five years of age, to take time to get away and refresh themselves. He went as far as to say he believed that in order for a mother of pre-schoolers to be her best, she needed to have at least one day out of the week to spend several hours by herself, away from her children. I think he made sure to add the "away from her children" part because he knew most of us would just count naptime, or the hour Our children played by themselves as this time of refreshment.

When I read his words, I felt as though I had been set free. Suddenly I felt validated (instead of guilty) for the strong desire I had been experiencing to take a break from my daily, baby-centered world. I had felt all alone in this because some of the moms around me would always talk about how they could never leave their baby with anyone else, and how no other person could possibly be trusted to care for their child. I, on the other hand, was starting to get so buggy inside my house I knew I needed to do *something* that would help me stay refreshed both as a mom and a wife.

The first thing I had to get over (and this is one of the biggest mental hurdles for the stay-at-home mom) is the cost of childcare. Now that I had quit my job, I had a bit of residual guilt over no longer contributing to the household finances. So to *pay* someone to come in and do the job I was supposed to be doing was difficult for me, kind of like I was having a double negative impact to the family. But I realized I was so exhausted all the time my attitude could sometimes be the real "double negative" to my family. After expressing my thoughts with Stovall, he was more than willing to pay for a babysitter once a week so that I could take the time needed to recharge and refresh myself.

Of course, the money to cover the sitter had to come from somewhere, which meant saying "yes" to the finances for the sitter and saying "no" to other things. We had to cut back on other areas of our budget and I took occasional extra writing jobs to make up the difference. But for me, it was worth the additional effort because it gave me the time to be proactive, rather than reactive, in planning my weeks. At the time, the going rate for a babysitter for one child was $6 per hour, $36 per week, about $145 per month. My average writing project earned $300, so one more project per month more than covered the cost.

The bottom line was that having some time alone to plan and to catch up on unfinished business helped me be more intentional about the way I lived my life. It helped me create margin in which to have real choices about how I allocated my time while Stovall was at work. And in those early years of marriage, he worked very long days. I knew I needed that time in order to stay sane, and I was willing to do what was needed to make it happen. I still think it is some of the best money I have ever spent.

If money is an issue for your family, please don't allow this to cause you to quickly dismiss the idea of childcare. I have seen women (including myself) become extremely creative in their strategies in order to effectively delegate home tasks. Some trade time, others tasks, others babysitting. Think of how you spend every dollar of your discretionary allowance. Do you get your nails done? Do you regularly go to Starbucks? Do you eat out? Ask yourself, would I rather get my nails done this month or do them myself and have a babysitter for a few hours? At first, you might not think you could possibly handle not having professionally manicured hands and feet or not having your daily Starbucks coffee. But for me, I craved some "me time" so badly, I chose to become quite proficient with nail polish and a coffee maker. However you manage it, I believe you will soon discover that living in the margins sometimes means you have to be very proactive to first create the margin you want to live in.

3. Create Systems. Order is extraordinarily important to me. In fact, it is essential in order for me to stay internally healthy. Not every one is wired like I am. I have a theory that motherhood comes more naturally to the woman with a more fluid sense of time and structure. Sometimes (many times actually) I wish I was wired that way, but I'm not. I'm a Type A Introvert who thrives in structure. So it's up to me to create structured systems in which I can thrive. This was crucial in my days of mothering preschoolers. Here are some tips for creating systems that will provide margin in your life.

Expect the unexpected. It's Murphy's Law. The unexpected always seems to come our way, along with the price of our precious time. One system I put into place is never to strive for filling every empty box on my calendar. "But Kerri," you ask. "The empty space in my daytimer is there to be filled, right?" Nope. If you would have asked me this before kids, I would have agreed with you. But now, I realize the need for that empty box, because weekly and sometimes daily, *something* unexpected arises—a run to the doctor, an errand for something to be repaired, or the worst emergency of all, you realize you really don't have an extra box of diapers and your baby just filled the last one. Today I intentionally leave boxes open and unscheduled, and I guard it faithfully, just so I have the margin to take care of the inevitable issues that are sure to come when you are building a family.

Learn to shift your weight. We all talk about how to achieve the elusive "balanced life." But if you think about the act of balancing, you will notice that the core skill needed is the ability to continuously, and almost imperceptibly, shift your weight. Learning balance in life is no different. Once you have simplified as much as you can, the next step is learning to adjust the weight of your attention and efforts toward the areas of life that need it at any given time. Sometimes the arena of "wife" needs a little more attention, so you lean in there. Sometimes the arena of "Mommy" needs more weight, so you balance your efforts in that direction. You get the picture. The truth is, you can't do everything with equal force and intensity at all times, so you need to learn to shift your force and intensity to the most important arenas on any given day and let the others areas lag behind momentarily.

Build Your Ability to Plan Long-Range. If you tend to look at your calendar day to day, try to look at it week to week. If you currently plan on a weekly basis, try to plan two weeks out. Make it your goal to have a flexible plan for a month and a firm plan two weeks. Having a firm plan doesn't mean having an inflexible plan; it just means that as far as you are involved, the loose ends are tied up. For example:

- You know what supplies your child needs for their school project and you have a plan to get them and place them in the backpack the night before they are due.
- You know what items you are supposed to bring to the potluck dinner at church.
- You know what you are wearing for your husband's birthday dinner, and you have time to get it dry cleaned or altered as needed.

The ability to look ahead on your calendar and think through the details of what is scheduled will help keep you proactive and not reactive when it comes to shaping your life.

Do Things in Chunks of Time. You might not realize it, but every time you switch tasks you lose time in transition. For example, if you run errands, pay bills, work out, do lunch and go grocery shopping on the same day, you lose time each time you transition between those tasks. I try to group types of tasks together. I know this might sound a little silly or neurotic, but I have noticed that different types of tasks require different kinds of energy. Relationship investment requires a different mindset and energy output than paying bills and household management. Grocery shopping and errands require a different energy output than long-range household planning, and all of those things require different energy than what I do at work. So as I strategize my long-term planning from week to week, I try my best to group tasks into similar output categories to ride the momentum of that particular energy. I schedule meetings with friends, pastoral care calls and visits, and dinner with church members on the same day. I schedule menu planning, long-range planning, and calendar planning, in the morning of one day, and errands and grocery shopping in the afternoon. When I am at work, I schedule input tasks, such as studying and research, together, and output tasks, such as meetings and training, on the same day. Writing gets it own day. As a result, I'm able to accomplish more on any given day during the allotted naptime slots.

Simplify. Childcare. Create Systems. These three strategies will help you learn to live life in the margins. Once you have kids, things can get crazy if you let them and your schedules can quickly spiral out of control. And that's never fun. We must keep in mind that the Bible tells us children are a *blessing* from the Lord, and that God's desire for every one of us is that we enjoy our lives. In other words, we can love and enjoy our lives even when we are blessed with an abundance of spit-up and poopy diapers! But we will still have to be strategic and proactive to create the needed margin for our souls to refuel. Become proficient at weeding out those activities that are not essential for this new season, and make sure to carve out space for dates. Dates with your husband, dates with yourself, and dates with God. You'll never regret the effort it might take, as these times will be like kisses on your cheek from Heaven.

Thing #7

Step Back for the Right Perspective

I love going to art museums. Granted, in this particular season of life I don't have frequent opportunities to spend an entire day to walk around and take in great art. On the occasion that I get to travel to a larger metropolis like New York City, London, or Sydney I really enjoy a day-trip to the local art museum (while Stovall is at the nearest sports event, of course!).

One of my favorite periods of art is Impressionism. It's characterized by its short, thick strokes of paint that are used simply to capture the essence of the subject, rather than its details. When these masterpieces came onto the scene in the mid to late 1800s, they created quite the stir because prior to this time, paintings were shiny, extremely detailed, and meticulously painted so as not to notice the actual brush strokes. It's hard to believe that Monet, Renoir, and Degas were actually confronted by hostile audiences for their rogue, willy-nilly artistic styles. But this is exactly why I love their works. They're vibrant, imperfect, and emotional.

While I love to stand up close to these paintings so I can look at the artists' thick, quick brush strokes, it certainly isn't the best way to view their work. Up close, a canvas looks messy, even sloppy, as all the colors bleed into each other, and usually what I see doesn't make much sense. But when I step back to view the painting in its entirety, I can see the true beauty the artist intended. From this vantage point, I can assume the perspective he wanted to convey as he brought into focus certain aspects of a particular scene. With his use of light and shadows, he highlighted the details he wanted the viewer to be drawn to, and in doing so, he told a complete story. Up close to a famous Degas painting, I can barely make out the semblance of a ballet slipper; but when I step back, suddenly I can see the gorgeous scene of ballet dancers at a rehearsal.

What does this have to do with being a mom? Everything! And, this is the #7 Thing I Wish Someone Told Me Before Becoming a Mom: Stop Worrying! Instead, Step Back to Get the Right Perspective.

When we become moms and we hold that tiny bundle in our arms for the first time, we feel in an almost physical sense the weight of responsibility that comes with that baby.

So how to we deal with that feeling of responsibility? From day one, we obsess over every little detail that has anything remotely to do with mothering our baby. Everything from eating schedules, to sleeping routines, to physical development, to social interaction, to cleanliness, to making sure his bottles are made out of the right kind of plastic. We become like superheroes with freakishly keen microscopic awareness for our secret superpower. We pay attention to the tiniest fluctuations in any of these areas, and if we notice a variance, alarms start to blare in our brains as we rush to rescue our child from the dangers of whatever could be going on.

We also micro-analyze our every decision with that same freakishly keen awareness. We worry. *Is she growing fast enough? Is she growing too fast? Is he spitting up too much? Is this the best formula? Did he poop enough today? Are these the best diapers? Is this the right rash cream? Is this pacifier going to give her buckteeth?* (Never mind that she has no teeth yet.) And then we perform another complete analysis of the answers to these questions.

Don't worry. You are not alone. Every mom has been this neurotic. I'm just hoping that by reading this book, you'll stop this downward spiral sooner than I did and come to realize that it's all going to be okay Most of the details we obsess over are actually minor issues, but we tend to stand so closely to the canvas of motherhood that it's difficult to get a true perspective. However, if you'll pause for a moment and step back just a bit, you'll begin to see that it really is okay that your baby didn't poop today and that he'll most likely make up for it tomorrow with a ginormous blow-out. And your child will not be permanently damaged with long-term issues because you left him without a pacifier for two days in a row. And the world will not tilt off its axis because you missed a feeding today. It's okay. You really can take a breath and relax in the realization that you don't have to get every detail just right. Stop the madness, take some steps back, and look at the broad spectrum of your life as a mom. Peace will begin to settle in as you adjust your focus to those things that *actually* are the important things to "get right" as a parent.

Just as when I look at that famous Degas painting of the ballet dancers. If I stand too closely, all I can see is a slipper, and I miss the beauty of the whole painting. Likewise, if I stand too close to my picture of motherhood by focusing most of my attention on the feeding schedule, the nap routine, or whether the freshly pureed baby food is organic or not, I'll completely miss the big picture of parenting God is trying to paint in my life. His desire is for me to keep my focus on the complete life of this eternal being, remembering that He and I are partnering together to nurture an amazing person who will one day be released into the world.

So much of what we moms obsessively worry about has a minimal impact on the big picture; but, unfortunately, too many of us don't realize this until several years later. We can become so overwhelmed with scrutinizing the details of the details that we lose the joy of being a mom. I heard it said once that with your first baby, when you drop the pacifier on the floor, you promptly throw it in the trash and get a new one. With the second baby, you rinse it off before putting it back in his mouth. By the third baby, if the dog licked it off, it's clean. And while I'm not condoning the use of dog saliva as an anti-bacterial cleanser, I do hope to help you relax a bit by giving you some thoughts about how to keep a long-term perspective in your approach to parenting.

THE ODD COUPLE

One of the greatest influences in my life, on giving me a clear perspective about motherhood, was my maternal grandmother. Her name was Evelyn Gertrude Louque Boyle, and while she was the spiritual matriarch of our family, she was also down-to-earth, funny, and little mischievous. She wore thick glasses with silver cat-eye frames that had little rhinestones in the corners, and her daily uniform was a house coat and slippers from TG&Y, the famous five-and-dime chain that used to be all over the South. Most of the week, or at least every time I saw her, she had her hair in pink foam rollers set with Dippity-Do. She'd take her rollers out, put on a dress for Sunday church services, and then promptly put the rollers back in again on Monday. Her favorite things to do were to wake up at the crack of dawn on Saturdays and go to garage sales, to draw, to read the Bible, to pray, and to feed people.

Shortly after Kaylan was born, I was very lonely, especially in the afternoons. I swear 3pm to 5pm is the universal witching hour, and across the planet, this is the time when babies and toddlers are all screaming at the top of their lungs. I was the first of my friends to step into motherhood, so they were working and generally unavailable to visit and both my mother and sister were working. I was desperate to talk with someone who used something other than 100 decibel shrieks to communicate, so I decided to get creative. That's when my grandmother came to mind. We'd been close in the past, but as busy as I'd been throughout college and now marriage, it had been a while since we'd really connected. She was a widow and couldn't drive, so I was pretty certain she'd be available.

That first time I drove up, she was so excited to see Kaylan and me. She came padding out to the car in her housecoat and slippers. Thus began a year of the two of us becoming quite the odd couple. She offered me wonderful adult conversation, and in return, I'd drive her around on the errands she otherwise wouldn't have been able to accomplish. In all honesty, I got the better end of the deal, as time with her imparted to me her spirit of strength, patience, and (perhaps most importantly) her long-term perspective. And as a bonus, she had a habit of always cooking too much food, which she carefully wrapped and kept frozen in her freezer. Inevitably, she'd send me home with a homemade meal.

My grandmother had a gentle way of helping me step back and look at the big picture. When I'd get freaked out about Kaylan crawling around and getting her clothes dirty, she'd casually respond, "Oh, don't worry. You can just wash that." And I'd think, *Huh? She's right; I can just wash it.* Or during our talks, if I became overly distracted because Kaylan was making too much noise with her toys, Grandma would say, "Oh, don't worry. She'll get bored with that in just a minute, here." And sure enough, Kaylan would soon stop. Or one time, when we were running late and I was coming undone at the fact we wouldn't get home in time for Kaylan to take her last nap, she'd softly remind me, "Oh, she'll be okay. She'll just make it up tonight as she sleeps." Time and time again, she'd see me getting uptight about something and would reassure me it wasn't a big deal. And you know what? She was almost always right. I didn't need to send myself into heart palpitations over the fact that Kaylan was getting dirty, being noisy, or would—God forbid—lose a nap!

You see, after surviving the Great Depression, raising four children, and creating a spiritual bedrock for her family, my grandmother little things that sent me over the edge. From her vantage point, as she looked out on the landscape of her day, she intuitively knew what was truly important and what was not, which things would matter in the long run, and which things did not. Grandma taught me how to step back, take my focus off the minor details I was amplifying into major issues, and view my world with a long-range outlook. "It's all going to be okay," she'd say.

My grandma encouraged me to slow down and embrace motherhood because laundry and work and cleaning and cooking would always be there. She laughed at the things that other moms my age were freaking out about, because she knew that in about a half a second, none of it would matter. She taught me to put love, forgiveness and trust before my own selfish needs, and she helped me honor and value this new part of my life. My time with her forced me to let go of my need to control every single day and freed me from obsessing over every single concern about raising my baby. Spending time with Grandma was the best thing that could have ever happened to me during this time.

Shortly after Kaylan's first birthday, Stovall and I moved to Jacksonville to start Celebration Church. Though we were too far to regularly visit, I will forever treasure those precious times with my grandmother. So much of what I gleaned from her life experience and her words of wisdom was timeless in its appeal and application. Through our renewed relationship

I learned that generations standing together are stronger than generations standing alone.

Long-term perspective like my grandmother had cannot be garnered from peer relationships or friends who share in your same season of life. If you don't have a strong Christian woman as a mother, a mentor or a friend, I urge you to take some time to pray about finding one. These mature relationships are integral as we walk through marriage and motherhood, as they offer us a viewpoint from a few thousand feet higher up the mountain of life. If you ask Him, God will provide someone who can be an influence on your life. If you open up your eyes and heart, you might be very surprised at who God brings across your path.

SO WHAT REALLY MATTERS?

My grandmother had such a handle on what really mattered and what didn't. And how she succeeded in this is exactly what this chapter is all about. She'd stop, take a step back, look at a problem from a broad (often eternal) point of view, and evaluate its level of importance. Over the course of her lifetime this process had become second nature. But for me, the "stop and breathe" technique was a skill I had to learn and become adept at practicing. When I found myself frustrated or ready to blow up, I learned to stop what I was doing, breathe, and take a mental step back to reevaluate things. I'd ask myself: Does this issue affect the character of my child? Is this an issue that in any way could cloud his view of salvation? Does the result of this issue harm anyone in any way, emotionally or physically?

Obviously, I could list several more, but I think you get the spirit of the kind of big picture questions I'd ask. And you know what? I still ask those same questions today.

For instance, during that first year with Kaylan, I had a book that offered a monthly list of particular milestones the average baby should hit. She should be able to hold up her head by X weeks. She should be able to pick up a raisin by X months. She should be sitting up by X months. This is exactly the kind of book I *never* should have bought because once I became aware of these milestones, if Kaylan didn't achieve each one at the proper time, obsessions would set in. Is something wrong with her? Should I call the doctor? What *exactly* do they mean by "pick up a raisin?" I'd worry so much, I'd practically send myself into a panic attack.

And then I'd remember Grandma. Stop. Step back. Breathe. Reevaluate.

Once I took the time to look at the *whole* picture of Kaylan's life, I got a revelation. So what if she doesn't sit up on her own at the exact time the book says she should? Does that mean she's not going to be as smart as the other kids? Of course not. And so what if she can't pick up a raisin with her thumb and index finger. Maybe she just doesn't like the way it feels. Does that mean she has developed some life-threatening neuro-muscular disorder? Odds are a million to one. None of these milestones are indicators of her personality or her character, so what am I so worried about?

By no means am I implying that we as parents shouldn't read books to educate ourselves, or pay careful attention to the development of our children and their health. I'm a firm believer of using every opportunity to learn how to be a better mom. However, sometimes we can get ourselves so caught up with doing things "by the book," whatever book that happens to be in your case, and we lose perspective. We take the precepts given in a particular program as if they are law, and we freak out if we can't make those detailed plans work exactly as the book commands. I found that whenever I was parenting Kaylan and was overcome with worry as I mapped out plans for her growth and development, I had lost perspective. It was time to stop, take a step back, and reevaluate if that plan was the right one for me *and* my child.

I also found that the only book that was a non-negotiable resource for parenting and giving proper milestones was THE Book, the Word of God. The Bible is full of valuable principles about how to parent, and when we understand and incorporate them into our families, everything else will simply fall into place. Once I learned to step back and gain a God-perspective of my motherhood canvas, I could begin to see the big picture and some crucial parenting principles that *really* matter. Here are some truths I believe can set the course for our children to hit God's milestones of character and wisdom.

1. Love God, Love People. Jesus summed it up perfectly in Matthew 22:37-40 when a man asked him what the greatest commandment was.

> *Jesus replied, 'You must love the Lord your God with all your heart, all your soul, and all your mind.' This is the first and greatest commandment. A second is equally important: 'Love your neighbor as yourself.' The entire law*

and all the demands of the prophets are based on these two commandments.'" (NLT)

If we will model this directive as parents, we will imprint this greatest commandment onto the hearts of our children. If the ONLY thing we get right as parents is to authentically teach them to love God and love people, then after all is said and done, they will be okay.

2. Stay Flexible. The parenting style you used for child #1 may not work at all for child #2. The discipline tactics that got super results with child #2 may completely backfire on you with child #3. This is why it's so important to regularly take steps back and reevaluate the landscape of your parenting. This is also why it can be unwise to adopt only one philosophy of parenting. When I look at my three children, they are all so remarkably different from each other; I'm amazed they all came from the same gene pool. . I've definitely had to be flexible with how I parent each one.

3. Relax Your Control. As much as we moms want to be in control of every moment of every day, have each moment mapped out so we can reach our highest level of productivity and raise the perfect child, it's just not going to happen. This relates to the principle of living life in the margins. We should live intentionally, but as soon as we've crossed over into inflexibility, we've lost perspective. We are no longer allowing life to happen, and we certainly won't be experiencing any amount of joy. Here's a fact. There are going to be days where nothing goes as planned. We can either drive ourselves crazy trying to micromanage those moments, or we can simply hang on and enjoy the ride. In the immortal words of Scarlet O'Hara, "I'll worry about that tomorrow. After all, tomorrow is another day." Only, leave out the 'worry' part.

HOW TO KNOW IF YOU NEED TO STEP BACK

Sometimes we need to take a step back from the minor details of parenting . Especially when we find ourselves out of balance. If you are losing sleep for all your worrying (Hello! You don't have much to spare!), you need perspective. Here are some of the issues I see moms fretting about that really aren't going to matter in the long run:

- Potty training - Your child does not have to be the first in his group to wear underpants. Even if he is the very last to step out of pull-ups, relax! He will eventually get it. Take a look around and you'll notice it is extremely rare to see a first-grader still in diapers.

- Codependence - "My baby needs to be with me at all times. Even sleeping." Do yourself a favor, and let this one go. NOTHING is going to happen if the baby is not with you. Not to mention, your husband will greatly appreciate not being kicked in the face by the baby as he is sleeping. In addition, you must realize that if your marriage is suffering because you cannot put the baby down, you've lost perspective.

- Sleeping through the night - So many moms worry about this one. Think about it—do you know any adults around you who have not yet learned to sleep through the night?

Relax. Your baby will get it.

- Breast-feeding - Depending upon where you live, there can be incredible pressure to breast-feed. Yes, I understand breast milk is best, but again, let's think about this. How many adults around you were breastfed? If they weren't, are they societal freaks? No. Have they grown a third arm? No. Does the Bible say that salvation is only for those who have suckled from their mother's boob? No. Relax. If your baby won't breast-feed, if your body isn't producing enough milk, or if you simply choose to bottle feed, it's okay.

And as for walking, talking, eating, sharing their toys, looking the person in the eye when they are greeted instead of burying their head in your shoulder, RELAX! Mark my words—your child will get it. Some sooner than others, but they all get a handle on these things eventually if you just keep working with them patiently.

In addition, there will be times when we need to take a step back from our own opinions. We've got to realize that everything that is important to you as a mom isn't going to be important to the mom sitting next to you. But this doesn't mean that *either* viewpoint is wrong. If we find ourselves judging another woman simply because she doesn't do things the way we do, we've lost our objectivity. We're standing way too close to the painting, staring at the ballet slipper. While one mom might feel the need to make every bit of her child's food by hand, another might feel just fine buying it from the grocery store. One mom might let her babies watch television while another chooses to forego this entertainment until they are older. Again, neither of these is wrong, they're simply differences in preference.

While you parent your baby, you'll probably choose to major on a particular aspect of parenting that your friend (or your sister, or your mother-in-law) couldn't care less about. Try not to allow these differing opinions to cause a wedge in your relationships. It's just not worth it! Remember to stop, take a breath, and ask yourself if these things are a big deal in the broad scheme of things.

You know you need to take a step back and take a look from a new angle when:

- You are so dogmatic about breast-feeding that when you are around your friends who bottle-feed, you end up arguing with them;
- You are so focused on having an unmedicated water birth that you can't hang around those who choose to have their babies in the hospital;
- You are stressed out trying to incorporate every single parenting tactic you see your friends are doing.

When you find yourself hyperventilating over these kinds of things, instead of reaching for a brown paper sack, just stop, breathe, take a step back, and view the situation with a long-term outlook. You'll probably see that what you're concerned about is really not worth a panic attack!

Thing #8

There Is No "Right Way"

Let's dig a little deeper. While all new moms fret, there is one major worry that prevails over all the little worries that pop up once we become a mom. It's a distress that from time to time can keep loving mothers all across the planet awake at night. It's the number one parenting concern that spans across every age, culture, race, religion, and economic position. As a pastor and conference speaker, I've been asked countless times to offer any insight that might bring some wisdom and comfort with regard to this age-old question:

"How do I know, *beyond a shadow of a doubt,* if I'm doing this motherhood thing right?"

Every woman (including myself) asks it. Every woman struggles with answering it.

I've researched high and low to uncover the secrets of solving this conundrum, and in doing so, I think I've actually found the answer! Though many mothers have wrestled with this question throughout the millennia of history to no avail, I am happy to report that the search can end. I have discovered the answer.

Are you ready? Are you *sure* you want to know the answer? Because once you know it you can't unknow it. Okay, here it goes.

You... don't.

You don't know if you're doing motherhood right. At least not without a shadow of a doubt. As you walk through the many years required to parent all your children, there will never be a day when you will feel absolutely, 100% certain you are doing (or have done) everything perfectly.

I know this is probably not the big, spectacular, life-altering answer you hoped it would be. But then again, if you really think about it and let the *truth* of that answer set in, you might find that it's more life-altering than it appears on the surface. Once I came to the realization that there was no perfect way to parent, I was set free. When I fully absorbed the revelation that there is no magic checklist of perfection to mark off to ensure a perfect outcome, I was finally able to take the enormous weight of perfect parenting off my shoulders. And I came to understand that this question wasn't necessarily the most important question I could ask.

So I stopped asking, "How do I know if I'm doing this *right,*" and started asking, "How can I, Kerri Weems, be the best mom God called *me* to be?" One of my dear friends helped me understand this concept in my early years of motherhood.

Once Kaylan was born, I spent many church services in Stovall's office. The church we attended was small and the nursery was even smaller, if you could even call it a nursery.

At that time, it consisted of a single room for all the kids under four years of age. It was supervised by one sweet grandma-type woman. Being a first time mom, I just couldn't bring myself to check my newborn into that small, cramped (though lovingly attended) room, so when Kaylan got restless and began crying during church services I'd go to Stovall's office to listen to the service while I fed the baby.

One Sunday, a good friend of mine, Kristen, had graciously chosen to sit with me in the office so I'd have someone to keep me company. That particular day, I was feeling very insecure about how I'd been performing as a mom. At that time, there were two very popular Christian philosophies to parenting. One had detailed plans and specific schedules about how to do just about everything, and the other was quite the opposite, with a much more loosey-goosey approach to raising kids. Pretty much everyone in my small world at this time had set up camp in one of these two philosophies.

And then there was me.

I had read the manuals, studied the processes, and while I found some really great applications for my life as a mom in each of them, there were also chunks of content in both of these approaches that didn't resonate. Whenever I've tried to implement those strategies, I wound up feeling like a square peg trying to squeeze into a round hole. So instead of committing fully to either, I took what I liked and forgot what I didn't.

But then I began to worry. I'd see other babies doing things Kaylan wasn't, and I'd start wondering that perhaps I should be parenting her differently. Or I'd casually mention to a friend that I had planned on enrolling Kaylan in our local mother's day out program once she was older, and while the friend wouldn't openly criticize me, the look of shock and awe on her face spoke volumes. Condemnation set in, along with doubts that I was being the "right" kind of mommy for Kaylan. What if *this other* mom was doing things the right way and my ways were wrong? The thought that I could be unintentionally short-changing my child filled me with anxiety.

In another situation, as friend and I were feeding our babies, I noticed she was spending the entire time teaching her child how to use sign language instead of allowing her to whine if she wanted more bananas. Meanwhile, my Kaylan was whining away. More condemnation, with embarrassment to boot. Should I be leveraging Kaylan's feeding time to teach sign language, too? Worry, stress, and more worry. I began to obsess that maybe this mom's approach was better than mine and that somehow I was failing at motherhood by neglecting to teach Kaylan how to sign "More bananas, please." The problem was, every time I tried to hop on the sign language bandwagon, we'd both end up tears. I was certain that at any moment, my nomination for "Worst Mommy" would arrive in the mail.

I shared with Kristen how terrible I felt, that I'd not been adhering as closely to these parenting books as some of the other moms were. I told her I had not been following a proper schedule for Kaylan, and how I kept missing the target times for her feeding/playtime/nap cycles. I confessed that when she'd wake up early from her nap and start crying, I'd go pick up Kaylan instead of leaving her there to cry until the allotted end time, as I knew I should. I knew I was breaking the rules when I let her sleep with me, after the middle-of-the-night feeding, just so I could get some rest I was feeling like a complete failure, and I worried that my inadequacies would somehow cause irreparable damage.

Kristen gave me a sideways look and said, "Where did you get the idea that you had to do all of that? So what if you go and pick her up when she cries? And as far as sleeping with you, sometimes you just gotta do whatever you gotta do to get some rest."

"Well," I said, "it's a book on parenting that I'm following. It's all about putting your baby on an exact schedule and keeping her there. It's supposed to train them to sleep through the night. Believe me, I could use a good night's sleep, but I just can't seem to stick to the program consistently. Most of my friends are doing the same thing, to the letter, I might add. I just don't know what's wrong with me."

"And there's no leeway at all?" she asked.

"Not really. The book is pretty adamant about following the program to the letter. There is another popular parenting philosophy right now that some of my other friends are doing, but that approach is totally not for me. It's all about forming an attachment with your baby. For the first couple years, you're not supposed to leave the baby alone or even with any other person. These people never leave their babies. *Never.* The baby sleeps with them each night, which makes me wonder how they ever had the opportunity to make the next baby? And at naptime, the mom will sit by the crib at just about the time the baby is supposed to wake up so that the very first thing the baby sees is her face. But I get so stir crazy sometimes, cooped up in the house all day long, that just going to the grocery store by myself is a rush. I can't see myself succeeding within those kinds of parameters. I guess I'm not naturally cut out for this mom thing."

Kristen let me finish expressing my frustrations. Then she said something that totally changed my perspective. "Kerri, that's great you are reading with books to help give you wisdom for parenting, and I recommend you keep doing that, but there is no one-size-fits-all way to raise kids. No matter what your friends are doing, you need to figure out what's right for you and just do that. God didn't give Kaylan to your friends to parent, or to the authors of those books. He gave her to you and Stovall. He knew all of her days before she was born and He ordered the first eighteen years of those days to be inside the Weems household. God has equipped YOU to raise Kaylan and to parent her the way you deem is the right way in this place and time. So, relax! And go get her out of her crib whenever you think its best!"

She probably doesn't know it, but that day Kristen taught me that God gave me my children to parent. And He gave you your children to parent. Not James Dobson, or Gary and Anne Marie Ezzo, or your super-mom, or your best friend, sister, or aunt. And not to your mother-in-law. He gave them to YOU. Therefore, He has uniquely enabled you to raise them according to His word and His purpose for their lives. While there are scores of amazing books available that can guide you on your journey of parenthood, as we talked about in the last chapter, there is only one way that can qualify as THE Way, and that's the Bible. And within the principles outlined in God's word, there's a huge amount of room for each individual family to work out the methods and types of parenting ideas that suit them best. If you will simply focus on becoming who God is calling you to be and on building your family into what He created it to be, then your specific style of parenting will emerge as the natural by-product.

THE NEED FOR STANDARDS

Motherhood is the Big Kahuna of important callings in life. Once we women cross the threshold of motherhood, it becomes such a core aspect of our female identity that we want to make absolutely certain we are doing it correctly. The only problem is that the many standards for success in motherhood are intangible. Can we confidently assume that the methods we used when our children were babies (and on into the teenage years) are directly connected with their behaviors once they are adults? To some extent, yes. But if a child grows up and is extremely successful, does that prove his mom was extremely successful? If he is only marginally successful, does that equate to a marginally successful mom? If he chooses not to serve God, does that mean his mom was a failure? Do we as parents bear the full weight of how our kids turn out? Haven't we seen ample exceptions both ways? As much as we would like for there to be a concrete, foolproof process of evaluating the effectiveness of our parenting methods, there just isn't one. And even if there were, we would have to wait twenty years or more to find out how we did. And even if we messed it all up,

127

we couldn't go back and fix it.

All the same, who wants to have gray areas in the parenting arena? We want black and white, quantifiable measures to let us know we are doing a good job. We want specific standards of measurements we can follow so we can have the assurance our kids aren't going to end up spending hours of their weeks lying on a therapist's couch. To make sure this doesn't happen, we obsessively search for the quintessential parenting advice from the latest and greatest parenting guru. We read the books and apply their detailed strategies for the day-to-day raising of our kids. Everything from sleep patterns, to exactly how and when to feed, from how and when to discipline, to how to magically decipher each cry, and even how and when to change diapers— it's all figured out for us. If we just follow the program, then *phew* everything is going to work out just fine.

The anxiety enters, however, when we allow ourselves to become so sold out to whatever ideology we are following that we become slaves to it rather than simply using that philosophy to guide us into our own discovery of motherhood. In essence, we begin to defer our parenting choices to someone else just because they've published a *New York Times* best-seller. This was precisely why I felt so condemned and insecure about my parenting that Sunday morning in Stovall's office. It wasn't until Kristen spoke those words of wisdom to me that I realized I'd been binding myself to someone else's way of parenting, stressing myself out as I tried to perfectly follow their teaching.

Obviously, I'm not saying we shouldn't educate ourselves (I'm the queen of research about everything pertaining to life, love, and happiness). And the entire book of Proverbs teaches us to, above all, seek wisdom and gain understanding. What I *am* saying, however, is we need to be careful that when we do engage in parenting programs and philosophies, we take the principles that are congruent with the values and dynamics of our individual family and chuck the ones that aren't!

Parenting styles and trends fluctuate from decade to decade. Some theories stand the test of time and others don't. The popular parenting styles of one generation often become obsolete for the next. One decade, all the books promote spanking as a discipline and the next, it's considered child abuse. In one era, parents are encouraged to micromanage their children's every move and in another, it's all about a hands-off approach. Parenting trends come and go, but believe it or not, humanity successfully forges on. When all is said and done, it seems the best option for finding quantifiers for motherhood is to arm ourselves the best we can and apply the wisdom and strategies that work for our unique home, in our particular time and space.

Even as you read this book, my desire is that you to take these suggestions and use them as a guide, *not* make a doctrine out of them. Even though these tips brought positive results in my life, don't use my story as a standard by which to compare your experience. Instead, utilize the ideas that resonate with you. And the rest? Just let them go. Remember, God gave your children to YOU to raise in the nurture and admonition of the Lord. And as you make God's Word your primary resource, you'll find solid footing as you navigate this thing called motherhood.

As you find your own parenting "zone," I want to share

with you some of the biblical principles that we focus on in the Weems household.

TRUE STANDARDS
Proverbs 24:3-4 says,

> *Through skillful and godly wisdom is a house (a life, a home, a family) built, and by understanding it is established [on a sound and good foundation], And by knowledge shall its chambers [of every area] be filled with all precious and pleasant riches.* (AMP)

While parenting trends may come and go, God's wisdom stands the test of the ages. His eternal and immutable wisdom is available to you as you seek to frame the structure of your "house." I love that the Amplified version of the Bible fleshes out the shades of meaning of that word, because back then a house truly meant more than the simple structure we think of today. To the princes and nobles of the ancient near east (who were the intended readers of Proverbs), the word house contained implicitly within it the notion of their family dynasty, their legacy, and the legacy of all of their ancestors. The task of "building the house" was placed in the hands of these young nobles, and it was no small responsibility. Without a doubt, it required incredible wisdom, understanding, and knowledge.

It is no different for us today. We know in our deepest hearts that we all desire much more than four walls and a roof as we frame out our house. We desire a home, a family, a legacy and all the significance they bring. These are all good,

God-given desires, and I am beyond grateful that He gives His wisdom to guide us as we construct our parenting path. The principles outlined in the Word of God are truths that will firmly stand the test of time. Throughout the Bible God paints a picture, sometimes in very broad strokes and sometimes in explicit detail, of the best possible plan for a healthy, thriving family. When God's Word is consistently applied, it will always produce great fruit. Of course, sometimes that fruit takes many years to mature, but we can be confident as we wait for that fruit to appear – God's word never fails us!

As we covered in Chapter 2, when we establish our core values, we begin to see a clearer picture of our identity. It's the same thing with parenting. To have confidence in the YOU God gave your children to, you must determine your core values for motherhood and family. When these core values align with the principles of God's Word, then you'll navigate family life from a position of confidence and strength. And your worries about "How do I know if I'm doing this thing right?" will begin loosen their hold on your thought life.

As I studied the Word of God, there were truths that resonated with me; ones that both Stovall and I were determined to make core values for our family. These non-negotiables have become pillars for our family life. The first principle I'll share is needed for the success of *every* family unit, but the others are the Biblical principles that are priority for the Weems household in particular.

Marriage First. Marriage was God's idea, as it was the very first covenant He established on earth. In the Book of Genesis, we read how God brought together a man and a woman, ordained them a family, and saw it was very good. And He didn't wait until children entered the picture to put His stamp of approval on the family unit. Marriage comes first, then kids, and when the kids grow up and move out, marriage remains "until death do us part." Stovall and I believe that above all, our marriage must be our priority. It is the central relationship of our family. The success and health of our marriage impacts the success and health of every other area of our family life. More than any other thing, the health of our marriage impacts the health of our kids and therefore is linked to our success as parents.

Please understand my heart here. I am in no way condemning those who are struggling in their marriages or walking through a divorce. I cannot even begin to recount the instances where I have seen the grace of God make up the difference in the lives of children affected by divorce. In fact, that would be a lot of our church family. I have loads of friends who are incredible single moms, whose kids are happy thriving, and positioned for a great future. This is the grace of God at work. But even these friends would tell you the impact of an unhealthy marriage goes way beyond the couple and presents you with obstacles that are difficult to overcome— difficult, but possible, with God.

I say all this to stress the importance of nurturing and guarding your marriage above all else. Sometimes saying yes to time with your spouse can mean saying no to time with your kids. This gets even more complicated as they get older. But remember that in choosing to nurture your marriage, you are nurturing your kids. If your marriage is strong and secure, then your children will have a firm footing upon which to build their own lives. If it is weak, unbalanced, and shaky, then your kids will feel the tension and insecurity. Notice I didn't say "perfect." No marriage is perfect, just as no parent is perfect. But if Stovall and I are both seeking truth as our marriage grows through the seasons of life, our children will thrive in the strength that comes from that solid foundation.

Honor and Respect. This is a non-negotiable in the Weems household. Stovall and I respect each other, the kids respect us, *and* the kids respect each other. It's easy to say we love one another, but the proof is in the pudding by how we treat each other. This is where respect comes in. When we operate with an attitude of consideration and deference toward each other, there is peace. We don't throw around the word "hate" at each other; there is no name-calling or even belittling speech toward each other. Both Stovall and I believe that the home is the starting line for Jesus' command to "love your neighbor as yourself." Just as it is important to instill respect for the authority inside the home, it's important to establish this respect for authority outside the home as well. We also don't allow complaining about teachers, coaches, pastors, or other leaders. We all know that children do what their parents *do,* NOT only what they *say* to do. Therefore, as parents, we need to make sure we are refraining from complaining about their outside authority figures as well.

Order. This one is huge for me. I am a firm believer that order and structure are very important, both for kids and for the sanity of the mom. I'll go to the grave believing that the best and most healthy way to parent is to give your child a sense of structure and order in their day. Granted, "structure and order" take on a different level of obsessiveness with me. I am by nature a very organized individual, and I am at my best when organizational systems are firmly in place. For instance, if you want a picture into my psyche, you need not look farther than my pantry. The cans are all stored according to food groups (i.e. fruit, vegetables, soups, or meats), with all the labels facing out. The jars are on separate shelves because, clearly, God intended that aluminum and glass should not dwell together. The boxed food has its own section, and the bagged chips have their own section. Everything has its place.

And so it goes with our household's day-to-day activities. Each day is scheduled and written down for everyone to see, meal plans are predetermined each month, and there are generally accepted rules of behavior by which we abide. The Weems household cruises peacefully within these parameters. While we are never religiously bound to what's written on the calendar, as spontaneous events and errands are inevitable, this basic structure keeps our lives from slipping into chaos. Obviously, what "order" means to me may not be what "order" means to you. There's room to be the kind of person God created you to be, so it's up to you to define your boundaries of how this plays out in your home. Within these basic confines, parents and children have the ability to flourish.

These three keys are a few of the core standards by which

our home runs. While I believe them to be the best for us, realize they might not be the best for you. Remember, God gave YOU your children to raise, not me. I'm offering these suggestions to you, simply so you can get ideas about how to choose the standards by which to frame your own family.

The message my friend Kristen gave me is worth repeating: There is no one-size-fits-all way to raise kids. No matter what your friends are doing, all you need to do is to figure out what's right for *you* and just do that. God didn't give your baby to your friends to parent, *or* to the creators of the most popular parenting movement. He gave your child to you and your husband. He knew all of your baby's days before she was born and He ordered the first 18 years of those days to be inside YOUR household. God has equipped YOU to raise your children and to parent them the way you deem is the right way in this place and time.

Rest assured in God's faith in YOU as a mommy.

Thing #9

Your Sex Life Will Never Be What It Was: It Will Get Better!

There just wasn't any way around it, so there was no point in trying to avoid the issue. Tonight marked the end of six solid weeks since Kaylan was born, so the allotted waiting period was over and it was time to rediscover conjugal bliss with my husband. Also, I'd already received official clearance from my doctor. It was time. I knew it. Stovall knew it. I knew he knew it, and quite possibly the worst fact, he knew I knew he knew it.

Everything in me wanted to delay this moment. My body had been through such tremendous and uncomfortable changes over the last, well, eleven months, and the very last thing I was looking forward to was having sex. In fact, I was feeling so physically and emotionally fatigued, all I fantasized about when I saw our big fluffy bed was sinking down into it and getting a full night's sleep, minus the three-hour feeding intervals.

And can we talk about what my body looked like? At least before the baby was born, my belly was nice and tight as it was filled to the brim with a human being. But after delivery—it was all wobbly and swollen, wrinkly and soft, and with enough stretch marks to resemble a street map. My muscles were still out of shape in places I didn't know could feel out of shape. And don't even let me get started on my boobs! Now engorged with enough milk to feed an entire orphanage, they were so enormous they could've been classified as weapons of mass destruction. Seriously, no one should have to buy a bra that large, especially when you're only 63 inches tall.

Furthermore, what about how my body *felt?* Until Kaylan was born, I didn't know such a level of exhaustion existed; the kind that hits you like a Mack truck and then clings to your every limb like a weighted blanket. I was in such a total haze, I really couldn't believe it had actually been six weeks, as my relationship with days and weeks had become totally estranged. Before babies, people have an innate sense of time simply by being awake during the day and asleep at night. After a newborn enters the picture, all bets are off. You sleep whenever and wherever you actually have the time and space to do this until the baby is on a solid sleep schedule. And that can take anywhere from four weeks to six months! By this point, I wasn't even feeling like a human, let alone acting like one.

It also didn't help that many of the other moms I had come to know had filled my mind with their horror stories about how awful sex was for them that first time after the baby was born. I won't even bother to pass their experiences along because I don't want to fill your mind with unnecessary fears that I soon found out were not the case for me. Suffice it to say that you should never listen to these types of stories because they only serve to freak you out about something that can't be predicted by someone else's experience.

Even though I had been given the green light, sex was the last thing on my mind. The big moment was inevitable, however, so I determined to just get it over with. I was nervous, I felt utterly unsexy, and I wished I could somehow convince my husband to give me another "6-week, Get Outta Sex FREE Card." However, that night I forged past my insecurities and physical fatigue, and without giving you a play-by-play (this isn't one of "those" kinds of books), I have to admit, I was pleasantly surprised.

And that is when we come to the #9 Thing I Wish Someone Would've Told Me Before Becoming a Mom: Your Sex Life Will Never Be What It Was: It Will Get Better! You might wonder why I would include a chapter about sex in a book about motherhood. It's because in our minds we tend to classify motherhood in a non-sexual way, which is funny because there is an obvious cause and effect relationship between sex and motherhood. Am I right? If you are anything like I was, then you have somehow gotten the impression that once kids enter the picture, sex is going to become mundane, difficult, and even painful at times. Perhaps, like pre-baby me, your expectation is that the sex you had when you were newlyweds (with your newlywed bodies) is going to be the best you'll ever have. I'm happy to be the one to tell you that you couldn't be more wrong.

Fulfilling sex (or frequency of sex) doesn't have to stop once you have kids, nor does it have to get less exciting as you go through your marriage journey. Granted, I need to stress it took intentional strategies on both my part and Stovall's to make our sex life great, but year by year, this realm of our marriage continues to get better and better. I want to encourage you never to give up working toward an incredible sex life with your husband. And, yes, that means even right after your baby is born.

SEX IS A GOD IDEA

Before we get into some practical strategies to help you keep this area of your life fun and exciting, I want to give you a spiritual perspective. For me, whenever I'm having difficulty engaging fully in any realm of life—marriage, motherhood, relationships—if I can zero in on some God thoughts for that area it helps me break through. When my flesh is fighting against God's ways, a spiritual mindset always gives me the ability to win the battle. And nothing in the marriage relationship is more spiritual than sex.

Did you know sex was actually an extremely powerful spiritual force designed by God to strengthen your marriage? Think about it. When God spoke through His Word to teach us about His relationship with the Church, He could have picked any metaphor by which to compare it. He could have chosen to illustrate how He relates with His people through the metaphor of Heavenly Father, or Provider, or any other aspect of Himself. However, throughout the New Testament, and much of the Old, God chooses the primary metaphor of a Bridegroom and His Bride. We read about this in the Gospels, in Ephesians 5:21-33, and again in Revelation 21:5, when the writer describes the New Jerusalem as "a bride beautifully dressed for her husband." In other words, there is no relationship, no covenant, more like God's commitment toward His Church than that of the marriage relationship.

Unpacking this truth further, the only place God has blessed sex to be sanctified and freely expressed is within the marriage covenant. Despite the propaganda the world tries to sell us, under no other circumstances is sex considered pure and holy before God. In addition, we aren't going to be having sex in heaven; it's totally an earth experience. So here's this element of life, completely exclusive to the marriage covenant and only existing in this tiny slice of human time. That's pretty significant, if you ask me. If we reduce sex to a bodily function that needs to be satisfied, then we're missing the power and point of it entirely.

Sex is a very spiritual and sacred aspect of marriage. I often hear women saying they wish their husbands would assume a more spiritual leadership role in their homes. This is because they underestimate just how spiritual it is when they allow their men to lead them in this arena. In addition, it is very likely that there is no place your man will feel more loved than during sex. Women can perceive love equally in other ways, such as in quality conversation, gifts of service, receiving presents; but, for the man sex is often the most powerful way he can give and receive love. As wives, it's an incredible spiritual privilege to share this intimate relationship with our husbands. So even right after having babies, when we feel the least interested ever about sex, we still need to muster up the tenacity to honor the important place sex has in our marriages.

How would you feel if your husband came home one day and said, "Honey, I'm really not that into talking with you. I'm not in the mood to hear about your emotions or about how your day went; it doesn't do anything for me. Basically, what I'm trying to say is I don't want to talk with you except every 4 or 5 days—that amount, I can totally handle—but anything more than that is just too much to ask." You'd probably say something like, "Uhhhhh, yeah. Hope that couch is comfortable because that's your new bed." I'm not trying to set forth some kind of legalistic standard to make you feel guilty if you're not having sex every day of your life, but I do want to give some thoughts about the significance of sex. Time and time again I've seen couples neglect this area and feel the repercussions of it in other facets of their marriages. Trust me, maintaining a consistent sex life with your husband is way more important to the health of your marriage than deciding whether or not you're in the mood to do it.

With that foundation lain, let's talk about some practical strategies for making this principle come to pass.

THE FIRST TIME
When the six-week period of abstinence is over, and it's time to get on with your normal marital life, there are things to consider. Let me prepare you from my own experience.

1. Ease up on the pressure. You're probably going to feel a little anxious, and there's nothing wrong with that. For heaven's sake, you just had a human being squeeze through a very small bodily portal! This is true especially if the delivery of your baby called for an intensive episiotomy. If you have any questions at all, I highly suggest having a detailed conversation with your doctor. For some reason I felt embarrassed to talk about the intimate parts of my body and life with my doctor. Crazy, right? However, had I done so, I probably wouldn't have been so freaked out about that first night back. Your OB/GYN will also be able to give you a realistic idea of what to expect, and that alone will take away a lot of the anxiety.

2. The first night back can't be a quickie. Take whatever time you need to relax. Talk with your husband if you're feeling nervous and let him know your hesitations. Again, for some reason this can be a bit embarrassing. Let's be honest, your instinct is probably to leave the actual medical events that occurred down there outside the bedroom. But there is no way for your husband to relate to your anxiety about sex if he doesn't know WHY the anxiety is there in the first place. Don't put pressure on yourself to be romantic or have the most sheet-ripping sex of your life. Just doing it will be an accomplishment. Be prepared to shift the plan if, once you get into it, it's too uncomfortable. That probably won't be the case, but just having talked about this option beforehand will help take some stress away. Also, your muscles down there might still be a little bit in shock from all the recent activity; don't be alarmed if it takes several times (maybe even weeks) of trying before you're able to once again reach consistent climaxes.

3. I am not a sex expert. I just happen have a lot of practice with *one person.* So talk to your doctor, read books, and be in tune with your body and emotions. The first time back in the sack is not, I repeat, NOT, any indicator of the future quality of your sex life. It's just the beginning, so relax and give yourself some grace.

THE NEED FOR TRANSITION TIME

Both Stovall and I came to realize shortly after Kaylan was born that shifting gears takes time. It's *very* important for a mom of small children—especially babies—to have a time of transition at the end of the day. Until we figured this out, here is how the evenings would sometimes play out:

I'd give the last feeding to Kaylan, *finally* get her to go down and fall asleep, and I'd plop down into bed, craving some time for myself. No sooner had my head touched down than Stovall would roll over and give me "the look." I'd respond with, "Hold up! I have *just* laid down! Can you hold on for a New York minute?" And then he'd get a little irritated. And then I'd feel guilty, and I'd try to make it up to him with pity sex. Now, don't act all innocent right now, like you can't believe I just wrote that; we all know what pity sex is. It's when we go through the motions because we feel bad that it's been so long since the last time we had sex, but our minds really aren't that into it. Of course, it's not that fun for the guy because he can always tell when his wife's not fully engaged. Don't get me wrong—he probably won't turn it down—but it certainly isn't his favorite.

Ultimately, neither of us was fully satisfied, as this type of evening rated far below the kind of sex life God had designed for us. We knew we needed to work to figure this thing out. It took both Stovall and me quite some time to realize that all I needed was some transition time from "Mommy" to "Kerri" before I could begin to think about wearing the "Wife" hat and creating space in my brain for sex. Before baby, this was never even the slightest bit of an issue as I had plenty of both "me" time and "Stovall and me" time. I could easily make the mental shifts when needed, and I never dreamed there would come a day when I'd want to give up sex just so I could get a few more minutes of sleep. But once Kaylan arrived, sleep and my alone time became such precious commodities, I found I readily wanted to make any sacrifices needed to allow me some time and space just for myself. And while it is *very* important moms figure out how to find these margins, it cannot be to the detriment of the intimate times we spend with our husbands. This concept is one of the biggest take-aways I hope you get from this chapter. This simple truth can prevent you from so many frustrations with kids as well as many arguments with your spouse.

There were several dynamics that accompanied our first baby's arrival that I was unprepared for. First, all day, every day, there was this tiny human being attached to my body who needed me for every single thing. Almost 24/7, I would pour into Kaylan emotionally, mentally, and physically (as I was the onsite lactating cow). Those first months consisted of complete sacrificial giving from me to her, as I was getting next to nothing in return. By the end of each day, I had given all I had in me to give.

Then Stovall would walk in the door. I'd feel so wrung dry, that I simply saw him as another person who ultimately was going to need something from me. But since I felt as though I had nothing left to give, as soon as he'd so much as make the slightest move toward romance, I'd give him the stink eye to ward him off. In addition, I had a newfound *very* intense emotional need to be alone. I felt guilty about it, but once Stovall got home, all I'd want to do is hand the baby off and lock myself away in a room where nobody could find me. What I didn't realize at first was that is *exactly* what I needed to do. Luckily, we figured this out before too much time passed, and I learned the tremendous fulfillment of having a bit of alone time at the backend of each day. It didn't take long before I felt like a new woman.

Nowadays, when I get questions about sex from a new mom, the first thing I recommend is for her to have conversation with her husband about the importance of transition time. For many moms, in those first several weeks and months, motherhood simply does not pour back into her, at least not to the same proportions as she is giving out. With a baby, it is PURE give, from time, to sleep, to attention, to physical exertion, to emotions. By the end of a day of serving another little person like this, all you want is to have some time to yourself to fill back up, however that might look. Some want to read, some want to paint, some want to have adult conversation. We need to have that time to transition from being Mommy (a *very* nonsexual role) to Woman. Just by taking an hour or so each evening to refresh yourself, you'll begin to awaken that Woman side of you and the Wife role (and all that goes with that) will be much easier to embrace.

IGNORING THE EXCUSES

You're tired. You feel fat. You feel overwhelmed. You're tired. You're emotionally spent. You haven't showered in a week. You have a headache. Oh yeah, and you're very, very, very tired. These may be legitimate excuses, but you cannot keep making excuses for why you don't want to have sex. Once you allow yourself to succumb to this habitual way of thinking, it can become really difficult to find your way out of it. You'll spend the rest of your life cleverly manipulating your day to avoid sex. Deal with the excuses now, and your marriage will be much happier for it.

You're tired. Yes, you are... and you are going to be for the next eighteen years. As moms, we must learn how to do "tired" well, otherwise that feeling will rule over us and convince us to make all kinds of unhealthy choices. Yes, we're tired. We need to just get over it. There are copious amounts of information about how to combat tiredness. Work out. Eat right. Understand your body and how different foods affect it. Limit sugar. Take some time and learn about the best ways to reenergize yourself.

And as far as sex goes, our husbands are more important than our feelings of tiredness. We need to figure out how to have enough of ourselves set aside just for him so he doesn't feel he's always getting our leftovers of time and energy. Let's be honest, how long does it really take? It's such a small quantity of time to sow into your marriage a few times a week, especially when you compare it to the huge return both you and your husband will reap.

Put your tiredness aside, and make a decision to put your heart and soul into this sacred time with your man. Give yourself freely, and you will also be given to! Most of us waste more time than that on Facebook, than it takes to have sex. Give that time to your husband instead and you'll never regret it.

You feel fat. Yep, and you can stand in line behind the many millions of women who feel this way, too. Our husbands don't care, so we need to stop whining about our imperfections. I know it's hard for us to believe that he finds our post-pregnancy body as sexual as he does, but he *really* does. Here's how I can prove it to you. Get the kids in bed, take a nice, yummy smelling bath, go straight to your bed, and send him a text that you're waiting for him upstairs. He'll be there as fast as his legs can carry him. He just doesn't care about *how* you look; he cares way more about how you feel and your ability to express yourself freely in the bedroom.

You feel overwhelmed. You're emotionally spent, and you have a headache. Yes, yes, and take an extra-strength Tylenol. More importantly, talk to him about it. If you're having trouble focusing on sex because you're feeling overwhelmed by the many un-checked items on your "to do" list, discuss it with him. I've heard it said that a woman's biggest sex organ is her mind, and I couldn't agree more. Many times men cannot understand how important it is to us that the laundry is done, the dishes are cleaned and put away, and the house is in order before we can relax enough to engage in the sexual realm. I have found if I just express my needs, my husband is more than willing to help me check off these items, especially when he knows that he is freeing me up to focus on something that is important to him (wink, wink)!

Simply make a choice to rise above excuses that only serve to hinder your marriage. Your sex life can continue to get better and better, even as you have more babies, but in order to have that you'll need to ditch the excuses.

SPONTANEITY

Huh? What is spontaneity? I almost had to go look it up in the dictionary before writing this next section. But then it hit me, *Oh yeeeeaaaaahhh... riiiiight. I remember what that word means.* Once babies arrive, spontaneity gets placed on the endangered species list. But don't worry about that for a second because, in my opinion, spontaneity is totally overrated.

Many couples overvalue spontaneity when it comes to sex because they mistakenly have made the goal of sex to be excitement. The goal of sex is not excitement, or craziness, or how we can make each encounter hotter than the last time. The goal of sex is love. It is a God-ordained celebration of the kind of love completely unique to a husband and a wife. As Stovall and I grow together in our marriage, as parents, in ministry, in the good times and the bad, our sex gets better and better. Not because we're hanging from the chandeliers or pulling out the costumes each weekend; but, because, as we do life together, we're more in love today than we've ever been before. As our love gets deeper, sex gets hotter.

While it's important to have times when we get away from the kids for a night or two, and even to have special week-long trips with just Stovall and me, these occasions are more like the dessert in our marriage, not the meat and potatoes. And most importantly, just because sex isn't spontaneous, doesn't mean it isn't authentically passionate.

Will your sex life ever be the same after having kids? Probably not. It will more likely get better. And while those times of long, drawn out, hours of foreplay might (for a time) be few and far between, remember this—before you know it, those kids will be grown up and out of the house; your daily life will go back to being just you and him. You'll have more time for spontaneity than you'll know what to do with. Hopefully by then you'll have continued to become more in love than ever before. So, let the games begin!

Thing #10

Your Children Are Only Young For a Season, So Enjoy It!

I could tell the older woman was about to say the dreaded sentence. It was the last thing in the world I wanted to hear at this moment, and as her lips began to form the first words, my only thoughts were, *Kerri, why did you open your big mouth and tell this woman how you are feeling? You already know what she's going to say. She gives you the* same *speech every time, and all you do is get aggravated!* I closed my eyes and braced myself for "the speech." Sure enough, she emotionally delivered the familiar monologue, her hands gesturing to provide proper emphasis, and when she was done, she gave me the usual hug of encouragement.

As she walked away, I hoped that I'd been able to appear gracious as she had offered her advice; she was a wonderfully nice woman, and I knew she meant well. But she obviously couldn't remember what it was like to be in the Mommy trenches, raising multiple pre-schoolers. If she truly remembered how I felt at this moment—frazzled, exhausted, overwhelmed—she'd have responded differently. She would have empathized with my current condition, maybe even offered to come over and help for a bit, and given me a gift certificate to the nearest Ben & Jerry's. Instead, she proved beyond a doubt her motherhood amnesia by giving me the speech. And now, instead of feeling uplifted, I was just irritated.

That's when I made a sincere oath to myself never to do the same thing. No matter how old I got, I would never, ever, *ever* sit down with a new mom who'd just poured her heart out about how challenging motherhood can be and give her "the speech." No... Matter... What. I simply was not going to be that woman. No way, now how. Neh—ver.

Almost fifteen years have gone by.

And I find myself needing to sink my teeth into a big slice of humble pie, because that dear woman was completely right, along with the dozens of other ladies who'd also given me their version of the speech. Her words spoke truth, and my inability at that time to recognize them as such, didn't make them any less so.

So I'm going back on the promise I made to myself all those years ago, and I'm about to give you my version of the speech. Consider it a rite of passage for womanhood, a passing of the baton of sorts. And in my delivery of the speech, that has been handed down countless times from generation to generation, I will try to word it in such a way that does *not* aggravate you, but rather, brings you a sense of encouragement and hope.

The #10 Thing I Wish Someone Had Told Me Before Becoming a Mom... wait a minute, let me re-word this last one. The #10 Thing Everyone Did Tell Me (But I Wish I Would've Believed It) is this: Parenting Babies Is Only A Season... So Learn to Enjoy It.

I will wait a moment before I move on for those of you who just threw this book across the room, as you'll need time to pick it back up and find your page again.

When I was in the midst of mothering one, then two, and then three pre-schoolers, the last thing in the world I wanted to hear, *especially* when I had just shared with someone how frustrated I felt, was "Oh, honey, this is only a season, and it goes by so fast! Before you have time to blink, they'll be on their way to college. Right now, you need to make sure you treasure every moment." I'd listen to this as I was wiping the spit-up off my blouse from baby #3, while trying to keep track of #1 & #2 who were running around like Thing 1 and Thing 2 from *The Cat in the Hat.* The words seemed so condescending, not to mention useless. I'd want to respond, "How does that answer help me one bit right now?" Followed by, "And furthermore, how can you call ten years of raising babies and preschoolers a season?! A season is, like, winter. That only lasts a few months. But this motherhood thing, it's not a season, it's a *life!*" And this is not even addressing the question about how any sane person could possible learn to "treasure every moment" of being slobbered all over, spit-upped stained, and pooped on 24/7.

It was true that I felt that way sometimes, and there was nothing wrong with that. So I want you to know that it is completely okay for you to feel this way sometimes, too, as you navigate those tough, first years of parenting. But I also want you to know that those well-meaning women are also right, as I can now attest. I have long since stepped out of that MOPS phase and have journeyed into a whole new season of motherhood. At the time of publishing this book, my youngest, Annabelle, is close to entering her 'tween years, and my middle-son Stovie and first-born, Kaylan, are full-fledged teenagers. My desire is to give you some thoughts of encouragement so maybe you'll be better than I was about taking the time to enjoy the ride.

YOU REALLY DO FORGET

Probably the reason I'd get so aggravated when someone told me to make sure I savored every moment of motherhood—"after all, those babies grow up so fast"—is because I felt it wasn't going fast enough! Caring for three small children is all-encompassing. The need for Mom's assistance is constant. They need an adult to do *everything* for them. "Mommy, can you get me some juice?" "Mommy, can you help me get dressed?" "Mommy, can you help me brush my teeth?" "Mommy, can you open this for me?" "Mommy! I pooped! Can you wipe my bottom?" "Mommy, can we go to the park?" "Mommy, I'm hungry." "Mommy, I'm bored, can you please entertain me?" "Mommy, Mommy, Mommy!!!"

Not until children are around seven or eight can they accomplish by themselves much of the minutia. Is it any wonder we sometimes feel overwhelmed and underpaid?

Being a mom to small children is intense and very hard work. With the babies needing you completely and incessantly, it's a Herculean feat just to put dinner on the table every night. Surely, there'll be days (many days) when you feel the stress and strain from it all, and you'll want to somehow press the fast-forward button of life so the entire family can magically skip ahead a few years into the future.

I remember feeling this way more times than I wish to admit. When I was in the daily whirlwind of motherhood, there were many moments and potential memories I glossed right over because I just wanted to get to the end of the day and fall into my bed. But now that I'm on the other side of it all, I must tell you that you don't need a fast-forward button. Time will move fast enough, and before you know it, you'll be looking for a rewind button. Because you really do forget. After holding my babies for thousands of hours, I couldn't believe I'd ever forget what it felt like to hold them; but just a few years later, I have. I can't remember what Kaylan's weight felt like in my arms, or what Stovie's little unique wiggles and stretches were. After rushing through countless bath times, I can't remember what it was like to feel Annabelle's wet hair against my cheek or to smell that fresh Johnson & Johnson's baby smell. Now, knowing I'll have to wait many years for grandbabies to have those experiences again, I wish I'd have stopped way more often to breathe in the precious moments of motherhood.

The only way to truly relish the season of life you are in (and this truth can apply to any realm of life) is to purposefully value each moment as you have it. Once those moments are gone, you won't be able to recapture all the details of them again. So often my focus was "when is all of this going to end?" and because I was so busy stretching my vision to make out the light at the end of the tunnel, I didn't value the journey through the tunnel. If on those days I'd have stopped to take a breath and recognize the blessings that were set in front of me, I would have realized I wasn't in a tunnel at all. The love and laughter and fulfillment of seeing this amazing life bloom right before my eyes were there for the taking.

Understand, I'm not implying that you spend all day long stalking your baby like paparazzi and taking home videos of her every movement. You have a household to run, a husband to care for, maybe other children and even a job to attend to. But I am encouraging you to take some time each day to appreciate what you have and where you are, because it really is just a season. No matter how long each day might seem, trust me, the years will quickly pass. This time you have with your baby is important and significant and wonderful. Amidst the chaos, make the conscious choice to embrace it and cherish it for the blessing of God that it truly is. Soon the baby phase of your life will come to an end, and like me, you'll graduate to the 'tween and teen stage.

SO... HOW DO I KNOW WHEN THE BABY SEASON IS OVER?

This certainly was a question I struggled to answer for quite some time, and depending upon what year it was, my opinions would swing like a pendulum. I hated the uncertainty of not having a concrete answer. Today I realize I was not alone because, as a pastor, I am asked time and time again how couples can answer questions like, How many kids are we supposed to have? How do we know when we're done having kids? Do we have faith in God to decide how many children we should have and not be concerned about contraception?

The answers for these questions are unique for every family, and each couple will simply have to determine them together. However, I would like to offer a few practical thoughts that can help you along the way:

Dismiss your preconceived magic numbers. Before Stovall and I were married, we had the usual how-many-kids-do-you-want conversation. I broached the subject with, "You should probably know that I'm really not interested in having any children." His answer, "Well, I'd like to have six." To this my quick wit replied, "I know! Let's make a compromise; let's have four, and I'll have two and you can have two!" ("Of course you want six because your body doesn't have to be pregnant six times!")

Needless to say, we decided to get married despite our difference of opinion, trusting that God would work the issue out in our hearts. And that didn't take very long, since I got pregnant very shortly after getting married. It was not too long after we had Kaylan that Stovall said to me, "I'm not sure about having six kids... how about four?" Then, shortly after Stovie was born, my husband's stance was, "Maybe not four... how about three?" A few months after *that* it changed again to, "Ummm... Two is really good. I think we should just wait on God to let us know if there will be a third."

I tell you this story because before you actually have the babies in your home, it can be very easy to have preconceived ideas about how many children you want. And the stronger you believe in that magic number, the harder it is to change your heart to align with God's call for your family. It's not until you are living out the reality of parenthood that you can fully understand the commitment, the joy, *and* the weight of it. For some, they think they want huge families but later realize their capacity and fulfillment comes at a much smaller number. For others, they believe they only want one or two, and once they're in it, they find they are called to five or six. So the first step in discovering the answer to this question is to dismiss your preconceptions of how many children you *thought* you were going to have. God has a funny way of messing up our plans; nevertheless, He will never leave you in the dark. You can trust that He'll make His way clear to you, which brings us to the next thought.

God will speak to you. After having Kaylan and Stovie, I began to think that maybe we were done. Just about the time I was feeling comfortable with that idea, I found out I was pregnant with Annabelle. At first, I was shocked and, honestly, a little upset (remember, I was the one who originally said I didn't want *any* children), but soon I began to get excited about the idea of three children. I was actually surprised at how quickly my heart was able to enlarge to envision three kids. So, what began with zero kids, very soon became two kids, and now that I had fully adjusted to three kids, I was completely at a loss as to how many kids we should have. In my heart, I really only wanted three. But what if I was wrong? After all, I had felt satisfied with only two, but now that Annabelle was here, I couldn't imagine life without her in our family.

I started making the rounds with my how-do-I-know-if-I'm-done survey, asking other moms who were farther along in the parenting journey than myself. I was very surprised to hear many of them saying, "Well, now that you have three, you might as well have four. You and Stovall are already outnumbered, so one more really isn't going to make a difference. Besides, four is better than three because it evens everything out." Being the logical person I am, plus my OCD-ish need for order, the even number thing started to make sense, especially after hearing it so many times. But then my analytical self would chime in, *Really? You're going to bring another child into the world just so you can achieve symmetry? Is it a good enough reason to bear a child because you want your family divisible by two?* When I heard myself thinking about it that way, that argument seemed ridiculous.

A few weeks later, I was at a luncheon with some leaders in our city. I was seated across from a very prominent older couple in our state, a couple whom I admire to this day. When I mentioned that I might have to scoot out a bit early because Annabelle was so young and I had to get back to feed her, we got into a discussion about family and having children. They asked me how many children we were going to have. When I answered Stovall and I had not decided yet, but that we were probably going to stop at three, this couple went on to share their philosophy of parenting (or, more accurately, conception) with me. They insisted that God was sovereign in this area, and we should let Him decide how many children were to be in our family. If it was God's desire for us to have more, then we'd get pregnant. If not, then we wouldn't. It was as simple as that, and to approach the subject in any other way would be interfering with God's sovereign will.

Stovall was not present for this dinner, and it felt quite odd to be discussing such a personal topic amongst a tableful of people I had just met, so I asked if we could change the subject. On one hand, I strongly disagreed with the general "Let God Decide" philosophy about how many kids to have. While it might've worked for that couple, it wasn't a core belief for Stovall and me. I personally believe God preordained sex as a means for conception; it's a physical law He placed in this earth. Therefore, if a sperm meets an egg, then there will be a baby. Saying, "We're just going to have sex and let God decide if we'll get pregnant" is the same thing as saying "I'm going to jump into that pool over there and let God decide if I'll get wet." There's a word for people who jump into pools. It's called "wet." And there's a word for people who always have unprotected sex. It's called "pregnant."

On the other hand, this couple's words still weighed heavy on my heart. Was God using them to send me a message? I took this concern before God and asked Him if He was trying to tell me something, if I needed to open my heart to having more kids. Even though I *really* didn't want to have more, I certainly didn't want to close my life off from a blessing from God. I couldn't imagine anything worse than standing before God and finding out there was another Weems in God's plan for our lives, but my stubbornness or fear had stopped it from being. I was at odds with myself and in turmoil over this issue for many days after the luncheon.

It was only about two weeks later that God clearly spoke to me. I can remember it as if it were yesterday, as it was one of a handful of times in my life that the Holy Spirit spoke to me so clearly that it nearly sounded as if He addressed me audibly. It was late afternoon, and I had taken Kaylan and Stovie to the park to release some energy. The two older kids were playing, Annabelle was dozing sweetly in her little stroller, and a beautiful sunset was beginning to light up the horizon. As the sky turned from blue to violet, and the early spring wind grew cooler through my jacket, I felt a tremendous sense of peace. It was a fullness, a contentment that I couldn't explain. I prayed, "Lord, I am so happy right now, just with these three kids. I want to stop standing by the baby buggy and begin to play on the playground. I'm ready to move on, but if there is another baby in my future, I don't want to stop your hand or turn your blessing away. Please help me know what to do."

I continued praying quietly, thinking about life, when all of a sudden I could spiritually feel His presence like a warm blanket on my body. And He said these words to my heart, "You're released. You don't *have* to have more kids. If you have more, I will bless you. If you don't have more, I will bless you. You are released." Instantly, I began to cry. For the first time, since I became pregnant with Kaylan five years earlier, I felt freedom regarding this dilemma.

If you are struggling with answering this question for your family, be at peace. Just as God can speak to you about who you are to marry, what kinds of giftings He's given you, and even what choices to make from day-to-day, He will speak to you about this very important topic. He certainly isn't trying to keep you in the dark about your destiny; He wants you to fulfill it! The answer may not come as quickly as you want it or in the way or timing you expect, but His promises are sure; if you seek, you will find; if you knock, the door will be opened to you.

There will be fullness in your heart. After God spoke to me that day, a funny thing happened. Now that I was free from the bondage of my own legalistic fears and preconceptions, I actually was open to have another baby. For the first time, I felt true clarity about this issue, so I wanted to go back to the drawing board and reevaluate with Stovall whether or not we desired to have a fourth child. We talked about it for the next few years, never feeling a strong inclination one way or another.

Finally, about the time I was 37 and our youngest was almost 4, I needed to have definitive closure. I could see the next season of my life perched and ready to take flight, but if we were going to have another baby, I knew those desires would have to stay shelved for a few more years. Stovall and I had some discussions, along with heartfelt prayer; and, in the end, we both sensed fullness in our hearts. It was the same inner knowing that had led us in all other life and ministry decisions we had had to make. We felt complete in our family and believed we were at the perfect capacity for God's plan for our lives.

I'm glad Stovall and I took the time needed to feel this

complete release, and I urge you to do the same. For some people, this knowing happens pretty quickly, and for others it takes awhile. Wherever you fall in that spectrum, take the time to weigh this issue prayerfully with God until you sense His release. I guarantee He will speak to your heart.

YOU CAN DO THIS

Being the mom of a baby is everything people say it is. It's amazing, it's exhausting, it changes you more than almost anything else, it's fun, it's hard work, it's rewarding, it's thankless, it's humbling, and it's one of the most significant things you will ever accomplish. *And* it's only a season. While it might seem sometimes as if it's lingering for a lifetime, in reality, your kids are babies for only a small fraction of your entire life. So learn to enjoy it, even when it's difficult. Take moments each day to get lost in the wonder of your child's development as she tries over and over and *over* to sit up. Treasure the softness of his skin and tiny, tiny toes. Laugh as she attempts to use a spoon for the first time, or as she calls her "pacifier" a "pedophile" and screams her need for it in the middle of the grocery store. Because as quickly as these things happen, they become memories, and before you know it, they're on their way to college. You'll *never* stop being a mom, but you will stop being "mommy" to a little one. Make a decision to love it... even in the midst of the chaos.

Conclusion

You Can Do This!

Motherhood. I don't think there is any other assignment on earth a woman can have that can make her feel more schizophrenic than being a mom! One day, you may feel a tremendous sense of accomplishment as your child conquers a new milestone, and the next, you wonder if anything you're doing is actually working. One day, you can experience a perfectly scheduled day, able to tick off each item on your "to do" list, and the next, you're going to bed wondering if you even brushed your teeth that day! One minute, you will be crying from laughing at the hilarity of your child saying the funniest thing and a few minutes later, the tears are from worry as your other baby just got her very first sky-high fever.

Motherhood will make your soul soar with mountain top emotions *and* it will sometimes take you to depths of feeling you never knew existed. You will love it most of the time, but you will also have days when you really don't like how it feels to be a mom. It will challenge you, it will stretch you, and it will motivate you to be the best "you" you can possibly be.

But most of all, it is the greatest honor and blessing you ever will have received from God. Never forget that out of all the other 6.5 billion people on the globe, God chose YOU to shape and mold the character of your little charges! With open hands, He entrusted you with children—and remember, they are ultimately His children—to guide, to guard, and to govern as they grow into their incredible adult destinies. I realize sometimes motherhood can seem overwhelming; but, if the Creator of the Universe has faith in your ability to parent, then why should you question it?

Just keep in mind that the idea of the perfect mother is a complete myth, so all you need to be is you. And with your identity firmly rooted in Christ, you'll be able to navigate through all the tremendous changes you, your husband, your marriage, and your world will be going through once your baby arrives. You'll be able to sense if *and* when the time is right for you to go back to work, you'll learn how to embrace (and love) your new post-baby body, and you'll figure out how to shuffle your daily goals to fit within the margins of time motherhood offers. And when the worries start to keep you up at night, as you obsess if you are getting this motherhood thing right, all you have to do is remind yourself to take some steps back and get a better perspective on the whole canvas of your parenting painting. God gave YOU and your husband your kids to raise, not anyone else. So stop comparing and start relaxing by getting away for a bit on a fun date with your husband... and make sure that night ends with some romance. Before you know it, this season of motherhood will come to a close as your adult children begin embarking on their own lives of marriage and parenting... and so the cycle continues.

You can do this. God believes you can, and so do I. Let's build the next generation of young men and women who love God and who are chomping at the bit to champion the cause of Christ in their world!

xoxo—Kerri Weems